COUNCIL *on*
FOREIGN
RELATIONS

Council Special Report No. 91
June 2021

Ending Human Trafficking in the Twenty-First Century

Jamille Bigio and Rachel B. Vogelstein

The Council on Foreign Relations (CFR) is an independent, nonpartisan membership organization, think tank, and publisher dedicated to being a resource for its members, government officials, business executives, journalists, educators and students, civic and religious leaders, and other interested citizens in order to help them better understand the world and the foreign policy choices facing the United States and other countries. Founded in 1921, CFR carries out its mission by maintaining a diverse membership, with special programs to promote interest and develop expertise in the next generation of foreign policy leaders; convening meetings at its headquarters in New York and in Washington, DC, and other cities where senior government officials, members of Congress, global leaders, and prominent thinkers come together with Council members to discuss and debate major international issues; supporting a Studies Program that fosters independent research, enabling CFR scholars to produce articles, reports, and books and hold roundtables that analyze foreign policy issues and make concrete policy recommendations; publishing *Foreign Affairs*, the preeminent journal on international affairs and U.S. foreign policy; sponsoring Independent Task Forces that produce reports with both findings and policy prescriptions on the most important foreign policy topics; and providing up-to-date information and analysis about world events and American foreign policy on its website, CFR.org.

The Council on Foreign Relations takes no institutional positions on policy issues and has no affiliation with the U.S. government. All views expressed in its publications and on its website are the sole responsibility of the author or authors.

Council Special Reports (CSRs) are concise policy briefs, produced to provide a rapid response to a developing crisis or contribute to the public's understanding of current policy dilemmas. CSRs are written by individual authors—who may be CFR fellows or acknowledged experts from outside the institution—in consultation with an advisory committee, and are intended to take sixty days from inception to publication. The committee serves as a sounding board and provides feedback on a draft report. It usually meets twice—once before a draft is written and once again when there is a draft for review; however, advisory committee members, unlike Task Force members, are not asked to sign off on the report or to otherwise endorse it. Once published, CSRs are posted on CFR.org.

For further information about CFR or this Special Report, please write to the Council on Foreign Relations, 58 East 68th Street, New York, NY 10065, or call the Communications office at 212.434.9888. Visit our website, CFR.org.

To submit a letter in response to a Council Special Report for publication on our website, CFR.org, you may send an email to publications@cfr.org. Alternatively, letters may be mailed to us at: Publications Department, Council on Foreign Relations, 58 East 68th Street, New York, NY 10065. Letters should include the writer's name, postal address, and daytime phone number. Letters may be edited for length and clarity, and may be published online. Please do not send attachments. All letters become the property of the Council on Foreign Relations and will not be returned. We regret that, owing to the volume of correspondence, we cannot respond to every letter.

This report is printed on paper that is FSC ® Chain-of-Custody Certified by a printer who is certified by BM TRADA North America Inc.

CONTENTS

FOREWORD

Human trafficking—which the United Nations defines as the recruitment, transportation, transfer, harboring, or receipt of people through force, fraud, or deception, with the aim of exploiting them for profit—is centuries old but remains a modern-day problem of significant proportions. It is a wide-reaching practice, encompassing men, women, boys, and girls used against their will to perform labor and sex, enter into marriage, and provide organs. It is a problem that is endemic across the globe, including here in the United States, with an estimated twenty-five million victims worldwide. And it is worsening, accelerated by the proliferation of migration crises, global conflicts, and the COVID-19 pandemic.

Besides being a severe human rights violation and humanitarian crisis, human trafficking also affects matters of national security, economic growth, and sustainable development. The practice contributes to economic losses; the total costs of human trafficking are estimated to be as much as $21 billion, the majority of which is lost income due to unpaid wages. Profits bankroll transnational crime syndicates and extremist groups. The result is that human trafficking can destabilize nations, impede strong governance, and undermine sustainable development.

In this Council Special Report, Jamille Bigio, senior fellow for the Women and Foreign Policy program at the Council on Foreign Relations, and Rachel Vogelstein, Douglas Dillon senior fellow and director of the Women and Foreign Policy program at the Council on Foreign Relations, offer a valuable primer on the nature and extent of the problem, explain why it matters, and provide numerous viable policy prescriptions. They also deftly take stock of the frameworks currently in place meant to stop human trafficking, including the Palermo Protocol and, in the United States, the Trafficking Victims Protection Act; describe how and why these policies fall short; and suggest how governments, private industry, and the security and development sectors can narrow this gap.

The authors find that while the United States and other governments, international organizations, and civil society have developed a comprehensive framework to better define the problem and institute standards, those efforts are insufficient. To do so, they argue for greater attention and funding, better tools, more research, and stronger implementation and accountability measures. Bigio and Vogelstein provide an array of clear policy recommendations on how to develop more robust legal standards and enforcement mechanisms to combat trafficking and ways the United States and other countries can work independently and collaboratively to prevent, detect, and disrupt trafficking operations. The authors highlight the value of immigration reform, including a temporary work-visa system. They also call on the White House to develop a revised National Action Plan to Combat Human Trafficking and increase prosecutions of individuals, networks, and businesses involved in trafficking.

The good news, according to Bigio and Vogelstein, is that "this agenda can be accomplished with modest investment of time and funding and promises significant returns for U.S. economic and security interests." All of which is to say that there are numerous ways this scourge can and should be addressed by governments and the private sector alike. Bigio and Vogelstein's report offers an excellent guide for doing just that.

Richard N. Haass
President
Council on Foreign Relations
June 2021

ACKNOWLEDGMENTS

This report was informed by CFR's study group on human trafficking, a distinguished collection of experts from government, multilateral organizations, academia, and the private and public sectors. The group included a bipartisan collection of former U.S. ambassadors-at-large to monitor and combat trafficking in persons, whose perspective was integral to the report. The study group was expertly chaired by James Cockayne, an accomplished and respected thought leader on human trafficking. Over several months, members of the study group participated in meetings, reviewed drafts, and shared research and insights from their work. The group's input considerably enhanced the report, and we are thankful for members' participation. The views expressed here and any errors are our own.

We are grateful to our tireless program coordinator Haydn Welch and to Hareem Abdullah, Delphi Cleaveland, Erik Fliegauf, and Elena Ortiz, who provided additional support in the report's production. Patricia Dorff and Cassandra Jensen, from CFR's Publications team, conducted thoughtful reviews of previous drafts, and Will Merrow, from CFR's Digital team, produced the figures. A special acknowledgment is extended to CFR President Richard N. Haass and Senior Vice President and Director of Studies James M. Lindsay for approving and guiding this project. This report was written under the auspices of the Women and Foreign Policy program.

Jamille Bigio and Rachel B. Vogelstein

INTRODUCTION

Human trafficking is a form of modern slavery. An estimated twenty-five million people worldwide are victims—a number only growing in the face of vulnerabilities fueled by the COVID-19 pandemic.[1] Other global challenges, such as the migration crisis and persistent conflict, also increase its prevalence. Today, the practice yields perpetrators an estimated $150 billion annually, making it one of the world's most profitable crimes. Not only is human trafficking a grave violation of human rights, but it also poses a strategic threat to U.S. interests in national security by bankrolling operations for transnational crime syndicates and extremist groups; undermining economic growth by undervaluing labor; and impeding sustainable development by retarding human potential.[2]

Over the past two decades, human rights and labor leaders developed a comprehensive international framework defining the crime of human trafficking, most notably in 2000 with the Palermo Protocol to Prevent, Suppress, and Punish Trafficking in Persons, Especially Women and Children. That same year, the U.S. government enacted the Trafficking Victims Protection Act (TVPA), which was signed into law by President Bill Clinton, reauthorized in the George W. Bush, Barack Obama, and Donald Trump administrations, and emulated in countries around the world. Twenty years after these standards were enacted, however, human trafficking persists unabated.

To reverse the growth of human trafficking, new tools—and partners—are needed in order to better implement global and national anti-trafficking standards. Private industry should be held accountable for due diligence to ensure that supply chains are free from forced labor, and the financial sector should do more to identify and report traffickers' illegal profits. Leaders in the security and development sectors need to recognize that trafficking undermines economic growth and fuels instability, and they should expand their policies to address this crime, including within their ranks. Governments should deter traffickers and decrease prevalence by using sustainable development approaches that address root causes and pairing them with reliable apprehension and punishment efforts.

The U.S. government should lead on the global stage to advance this approach by strengthening institutional authorities and coordination, improving accountability, increasing resources, and expanding evidence and data. Specifically, it should enact due diligence reforms to promote corporate accountability for forced labor in supply chains; implement policies that combat the exploitation of migrant workers; increase trafficking prosecutions by scaling the successful U.S. anti-trafficking coordination team model, which includes law enforcement, labor officials, and social service providers; leverage technology against human trafficking; and increase investment to counter it. The Joe Biden administration and Congress should enlist leaders in the private, security, and global development sectors to propose innovative and robust prevention and enforcement initiatives, adding critical tools to the arsenal of human rights–based and prosecutorial approaches that have been underenforced globally and produced far too little progress to date.

UNDERSTANDING HUMAN TRAFFICKING

Human trafficking is an egregious and ubiquitous human rights violation. The UN Office on Drugs and Crime (UNODC) defines it as the recruitment, transportation, transfer, harboring, or receipt of people through threat or abduction, abuse of power or vulnerability, deception, coercion, fraud, force, or giving of payments or benefits to a person in control of a victim for the purpose of exploitation.[3] A truly global phenomenon, human trafficking occurs in almost every country, including the United States. Poverty, social marginalization, migratory status, weak criminal justice systems, and conflict all increase people's vulnerability to exploitation by traffickers.[4]

Several kinds of exploitation fall under the umbrella of human trafficking, which most commonly takes one of four forms: labor trafficking, sex trafficking, forced marriage, or trafficking in persons for the removal of their organs. Other forms of trafficking include the sale of infants, forced criminal behavior, and trafficking for exploitative street begging. The prevalence of the different types of human trafficking varies across different regions of the world (see figure 1).[5]

Among detected trafficking victims, most are exploited within their country of residence or are trafficked across national borders within the same region; others are trafficked across regions, the largest numbers being detected in Europe and North America (see figure 2).[6]

The International Labor Organization (ILO) estimates that there are twenty-five million victims of forced labor and forced sexual exploitation worldwide, but only a small fraction of these victims are reported to authorities. UNODC, which collects data on detected numbers of human trafficking victims, received about fifty thousand reports of human trafficking in its latest analysis. Women and girls

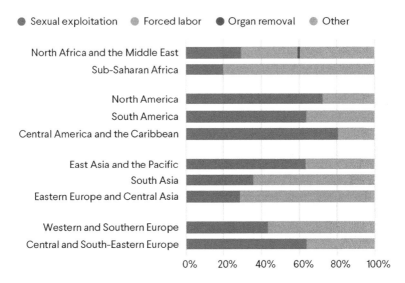

Figure 1. FORMS OF EXPLOITATION VARY BY REGION

Detected trafficking victims by form of exploitation, 2018 or most recent

● Sexual exploitation ● Forced labor ● Organ removal ● Other

Source: UNODC.

represent the majority of detected victims and are trafficked for sexual exploitation, forced labor, and other forms of exploitation, including forced marriage (see figure 3). However, the data is skewed toward those who are detected by official channels, and evidence indicates that women and girls trafficked for sexual exploitation are more likely to be detected globally than victims of forced labor.[7]

Although human trafficking is primarily driven by exploitative individuals or groups, some governments also fuel the practice by explicitly supporting forced labor and sexual enslavement or using child soldiers. The State Department in 2020 identified ten countries with a policy or practice supporting human trafficking—often for years, regardless of international condemnation: Afghanistan, Belarus, Burma, China, Cuba, Eritrea, North Korea, Russia, South Sudan, and Turkmenistan.[8]

Despite the estimated twenty-five million victims, impunity is widespread, with the vast majority of trafficking cases not prosecuted: the U.S. Department of State Trafficking in Persons (TIP) Report estimated only 11,841 prosecutions worldwide in 2019.[9]

Figure 2. MOST TRAFFICKING OCCURS WITHIN REGIONS

Detected trafficking victims, 2018 or most recent

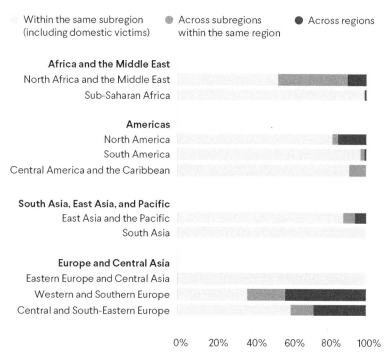

Within the same subregion (including domestic victims) ● Across subregions within the same region ● Across regions

Africa and the Middle East
North Africa and the Middle East
Sub-Saharan Africa

Americas
North America
South America
Central America and the Caribbean

South Asia, East Asia, and Pacific
East Asia and the Pacific
South Asia

Europe and Central Asia
Eastern Europe and Central Asia
Western and Southern Europe
Central and South-Eastern Europe

0%   20%   40%   60%   80%   100%

Note: Bars represent subregions within the four regions (Africa and the Middle East; Americas; South Asia, East Asia, and Pacific; and Europe and Central Asia).

Source: UNODC.

LABOR TRAFFICKING

Forced labor is far more prevalent than commonly realized. The ILO defines forced labor as "all work or service exacted from any person under the menace of any penalty and for which the person has not offered themselves voluntarily."[10] People of all genders and ages—including approximately four million children—are trafficked for labor in a range of fields that include domestic work, agriculture, textiles and factory work, construction, and commercial fishing.[11] Victims usually face extremely hazardous conditions and excessively long hours, and many also endure wage theft and coerced debt.

Figure 3. THE MAJORITY OF DETECTED TRAFFICKING VICTIMS ARE WOMEN AND GIRLS

Detected trafficking victims by sex, age, and type of exploitation, 2018 or most recent

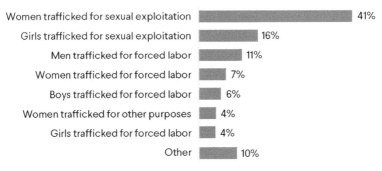

Women trafficked for sexual exploitation	41%
Girls trafficked for sexual exploitation	16%
Men trafficked for forced labor	11%
Women trafficked for forced labor	7%
Boys trafficked for forced labor	6%
Women trafficked for other purposes	4%
Girls trafficked for forced labor	4%
Other	10%

Source: UNODC.

Forced labor occurs around the world, but workers in the informal economy—approximately two billion people (60 percent of the global workforce), concentrated in emerging and developing nations—are particularly vulnerable.[12] Workers in unskilled, temporary, and dangerous professions also face a greater risk of exploitation. Migrant workers make up 25 percent of forced labor victims globally.[13] Labor recruiters often take advantage of their economic vulnerability by charging exorbitant fees to place them with employers in a destination country—sometimes in a debt bondage arrangement, under which a worker receives low or no wages to repay the recruitment debt.[14] Other recruiters fraudulently conceal the true nature of a job, leaving migrant workers, who end up in a forced labor situation; in some cases, for example, women are promised jobs in the hospitality industry only to find themselves held captive in domestic servitude.[15] And some migrant workers, fearing arrest or deportation, believe they cannot leave abusive environments.[16] In the Middle East and North Africa, for example, domestic laborers governed under the *kafala* system—one in which the legal status of foreign workers is linked to their employers—remain unprotected from abuse (see appendix 1 for more detail on labor trafficking in the Arabian Gulf and an additional four regional case studies on other forms of human trafficking).

Forced labor in conflict settings is a persistent challenge. In many regions, parties to conflict force civilians to work in construction, mining, and domestic servitude, for example, to support an armed or terrorist group.[17] Civilians fleeing conflict are also susceptible to fraudulent recruitment and debt bondage.[18] Forced labor of children—their use as child soldiers—is a war crime, and tens of thousands of children are thought to be fighting in wars today.[19] Children in war zones are especially vulnerable to trafficking because of displacement, separation from their families, or inability to attend school.[20]

Layoffs related to the COVID-19 pandemic only exacerbate the vulnerability of marginalized communities to trafficking and exploitation.[21] Workers living on the edge of poverty are more susceptible to the fraudulent job offers and predatory loans that lead to situations of forced labor and debt bondage.[22]

SEX TRAFFICKING

Although the ILO considers sex trafficking to be a form of forced labor, the U.S. government categorizes sex trafficking separately. According to the U.S. Department of Justice, sex trafficking occurs when "a commercial sex act is induced by force, fraud, or coercion," or when "the person induced to perform such act has not attained eighteen years of age."[23] The vast majority of detected victims are women and girls, but men and boys are sexually exploited as well.[24]

Both individuals and organizations perpetrate sex trafficking, which often occurs in brothels or private homes controlled by traffickers, where victims are not able to leave and can have their documents confiscated.[25] Sex trafficking also manifests in outdoor sex solicitation, escort services, and illicit spa services.[26] Rates of online sexual exploitation are also rising: In the Philippines, for example, between 2014 and 2017 the prevalence rate of online child exploitation more than tripled; in the United Kingdom, women trafficked from eastern Europe were sold via online ads for "pop-up" brothels in temporary rentals.[27] In 2020, the demand spiked globally as the COVID-19 crisis pushed more interactions online.[28] The internet also facilitates sexual exploitation in the context of travel and tourism, with tourists expressly traveling to areas where commercial sexual exploitation is common, as is the case with the resort and coastal areas of Brazil (see appendix 1).

Criminal sex-trafficking networks are often global. For example, an international organized crime network trafficked hundreds of Thai women to the United States for the purpose of sexual exploitation, generating tens of millions of dollars in illicit profits until U.S. law enforcement dismantled the organization and convicted thirty-six traf- fickers between 2016 and 2018.[29] Sex trafficking can also be perpetrated by the same institutions charged with protecting the world's most vul- nerable—for example, when national military, North Atlantic Treaty Organization (NATO), or UN peacekeeping personnel perpetrate this crime while on mission.

FORCED MARRIAGE

The Office of the United Nations High Commissioner for Human Rights defines forced marriage as one in which one or both parties do not give their full, free, and informed consent.[30] Worldwide, 15.4 mil- lion people are in forced marriages.[31] Early marriage is the forced mar- riage of a child under eighteen, which is the internationally established minimum age.[32] Although men and boys can be forced into marriage, women and girls are far more likely to be victimized in a situation that is tantamount to slavery, which requires the performance of unpaid domestic and caregiving work often while enduring sexual, physical, and emotional violence as well as isolation from family and friends.[33] Victims are more likely to come from impoverished homes and have little education.[34]

International organizations are increasingly classifying forced mar- riage—once thought of as a private family matter or cultural practice— as a form of modern slavery. Although no global consensus exists about the definition of modern slavery, the term is used to refer to a multitude of exploitative situations a person cannot refuse or leave, including forced labor, debt bondage, human trafficking, forced marriage, and other practices tantamount to slavery.

When the ILO categorized forced marriage as modern slavery in 2017, it recognized that millions of women and girls are being forced or tricked into marrying people who then exploit them for domestic labor and sex against their will.[35] In 2020, the UNODC released a report high- lighting the linkages between forced marriage and trafficking in per- sons, documenting instances where girls as young as twelve have been compelled into marrying men by family members, brokers, or kidnap- pers, frequently for material gain.[36] This practice spans the world, with instances of early marriage highest in sub-Saharan Africa and in South Asia, where around a third of young women were married before age eighteen (see appendix 1 for a case study on India).[37]

Forced marriage often increases in conflict and postconflict set- tings because greater instability and poverty incentivize parents to force their girls to marry early as an economic safety net or a method of protection.[38] During the COVID-19 crisis, the economic stress posed by the pandemic is expected to contribute to thirteen million more child marriages around the world as families resort to this form of child labor.[39]

Armed and extremist groups also traffic women and girls for the purpose of forced marriage. Central Africa's Lord's Resistance Army and Sierra Leone's Revolutionary United Front abducted women and girls as "bush wives," forcing them to marry combatants as well as to clean, cook, and sometimes participate in armed attacks.[40] The self-proclaimed Islamic State recruited thousands of male affiliates, in part by promising kidnapped women and girls as "wives."[41]

TRAFFICKING IN PERSONS FOR ORGANS

Human trafficking for organ removal takes place when traffickers remove organs from people through fraud, coercion, or force to generate revenue.[42] Victims are vulnerable because of their poverty and frequently unaware of the hazards to their health.[43] Migrants are at particular risk: for example, in recent years, traffickers have forced some African migrants fleeing conflict to sell organs in exchange for safe passage into European nations.[44] Armed and extremist groups also employ this form of trafficking to generate revenue and treat injured fighters.[45] The demand for organs is significant—buyers are willing to pay up to $80,000 for a kidney and $290,000 for a heart or lung—yielding hundreds of millions in profits annually.[46] Extremist groups including Jabhat Fateh al-Sham and the Islamic State have capitalized on this exploitation.[47]

IMPLICATIONS FOR U.S. INTERESTS

Human trafficking not only violates human rights but also undermines national security, retards economic growth, and impedes sustainable development, hindering U.S. interests in prosperity, security, and stability.

NATIONAL SECURITY

Human trafficking imperils national security by fueling corruption and criminal networks.[48] Trafficking in persons is one of the most lucrative forms of organized crime, yielding an estimated $150 billion in profit each year.[49] Given the steady demand for forced labor and sex work, as well as insufficient law enforcement efforts, perpetrators generally consider trafficking to be a low-risk and high-profit enterprise.[50]

Human trafficking strengthens criminal groups by diversifying their funding sources and expanding their activities. In Mexico, for example, several large drug trafficking syndicates split into smaller groups focused on particular types of crime, making them nimbler and more resistant to enforcement efforts.[51] Trafficking in persons also helps criminal groups augment existing activities—by, for example, forcing victims to convey drugs, thereby multiplying profits.[52] Routes used for human trafficking are used for other criminal pursuits as well, such as arms, drug, and wildlife trafficking. The implications for national security are significant.[53]

Human trafficking also undermines national security by bolstering terrorist and armed groups, who use forced labor and sex trafficking to generate recruits and revenue, enlarge military capabilities, and augment operations. Victims of trafficking are used in many capacities, from combatants and spies to cooks and messengers.[54]

Some extremist organizations have used human trafficking as a terror tool by targeting specific groups, as the Islamic State did with Yazidi women and girls.[55] The strategic and financial benefits that human trafficking affords enhance the power of armed and extremist groups, thereby prolonging conflict.

In repressive government regimes, human trafficking—particularly forced labor—is often used to foster economic gains or circumvent sanctions, weakening a critical national security tool. The North Korean government, for example, sent almost one hundred thousand forced laborers to work abroad, primarily in China and Russia, generating more than $500 million each year for the sanctioned government.[56] Other authoritarian governments use forced labor as a repression tool against certain populations or as a form of punishment, such as the brutal campaign by the Chinese government against the Uyghurs and other ethnic minorities (see appendix 1).[57] In 2016 alone, nearly four million people were entrapped in state-sanctioned forced labor.[58] Such abuses fuel displacement, further contributing to destabilization.[59]

Human trafficking also undermines international cooperation. The trafficking of women in and around military and peacekeeping missions, for example, both betrays the purpose of such efforts and decreases confidence in the international system. Between 2001 and 2011, studies showed a correlation between the presence of peacekeeping forces and forced prostitution.[60] Similarly, a rise in military presence frequently coincides with elevated demand for sexual exploitation. Consider, for example, the trafficking of women around U.S. military bases in South Korea—with women from China, the Philippines, and Russia held in bondage to traffickers—or in Yugoslavia, where NATO troops deployed during and after the Kosovo War in 1999 exploited trafficked women from Balkan countries, transforming a small prostitution market into a significant sex-trafficking industry.[61] Trafficking in persons committed or permitted by security forces weakens the integrity of international institutions and compromises their ability to execute their missions, undermining U.S. security interests.[62]

ECONOMIC GROWTH

Human trafficking imperils economic growth and the stability of global financial systems by fueling illegal and unregulated markets, putting legally compliant private-sector actors at a disadvantage and eliminating tax revenue from the government. In 2009, the ILO estimated the total costs of coercion to workers, excluding sexual exploitation, to be as much as $21 billion, including $19.6 billion in lost income due to unpaid wages—earnings that are excluded from tax coffers.[63] Although the profits of human trafficking are privatized, the costs are spread across society: one study shows that every human trafficking case in the United Kingdom costs more than 325,000 British pounds in direct costs, including for health care and law enforcement.[64] As to child marriage, International Monetary Fund (IMF) researchers calculated that emerging and developing countries stand to gain more than 1 percent in annual gross domestic product (GDP) if just this one form of modern slavery were eradicated.[65] Human trafficking is a market failure: overlooking its true social and economic costs leads to inefficient capital allocation, whereby enterprises that tolerate human trafficking have a competitive advantage over those that do not.[66]

Human trafficking also erodes stability in global supply chains. Forced labor introduces risks to investors, given the threat of supply chain disruption, fines due to factory closures or import restrictions, and other law enforcement measures.[67] Corporations that ignore or tolerate human trafficking in their supply chains face growing reputational and compliance costs, especially as some nations consider regulations that would mandate transparency or due diligence to identify and combat forced labor.

Human trafficking also exacerbates global wealth inequality. The rise of economic globalization has increased income inequality, furthering the conditions in which human trafficking thrives.[68] In developed nations, multinational businesses' growing demand for cheap labor has coincided with the desperation of workers who have lost their livelihoods to technological and other economic shifts, increasing their susceptibility to trafficking.[69] Government failure to protect labor rights, including freedom of association, has also fueled worker vulnerability to forced labor and other exploitation. Although all but nine ILO member states have ratified ILO Convention 29, which prohibits forced labor, far too few governments are adequately enforcing it.[70]

SUSTAINABLE DEVELOPMENT

Human trafficking impedes sustainable development, undermining U.S. interests in prosperity and stability.[71] Human trafficking creates a cycle of poverty, compounding illiteracy, poor health and nutrition, and vulnerability across generations. The human costs are long lasting: in sex trafficking, for example, women and girls who escape nevertheless can face enduring complications, including HIV infection, poor marriage prospects, or ostracism for children born of rape.[72] Those held in forced labor can face multigenerational debt bondage, which traps entire families in servitude when debts attach to children following the death of a parent.[73]

Human trafficking undermines sustainable development by destabilizing communities.[74] Fear of trafficking fuels displacement, which divests communities of human potential. In Central America's Northern Triangle region, for instance, some sources report that rising levels of gang violence—including violence related to human trafficking—contributed to their decision to migrate.[75]

Human trafficking also fuels corrupt practices, weakening democracies and impeding strong governance. Human traffickers encourage the erosion of democratic institutions, including by recruiting corrupt officials from police to customs officers to prosecutors.[76]

POLICY LANDSCAPE AND SHORTCOMINGS

Over the past two decades, multilateral institutions and governments around the world—including the U.S. government—have enacted a number of policies and programs to combat human trafficking, focused on stopping the individuals and networks that exploit this criminal practice; reforming the institutional environment; and addressing the factors that make people vulnerable to trafficking in the first place. However, despite this comprehensive framework, anti-trafficking efforts are undermined by insufficient authorities, weak enforcement, limited investment, and inadequate data. This failure impedes U.S. interests in national security, economic growth, and sustainable development.

POLICY LANDSCAPE

In 1930, the ILO adopted its first of eight fundamental conventions laying out international labor standards, starting with a focus on the issue of forced labor. In 1948, the Universal Declaration of Human Rights recognized freedom from slavery or servitude as a fundamental human right and urged the prohibition of slavery and the slave trade in all forms (see appendix 2 for a list of primary global agreements on human trafficking and forced labor).[77]

In 2000, the Palermo Protocol to Prevent, Suppress and Punish Trafficking in Persons—the first international instrument to define human trafficking—committed ratifying states to preventing and addressing this scourge. That same year, the U.S. government enacted the TVPA to implement its mandate. Signed by President Clinton and reauthorized in the Bush, Obama, and Trump administrations, the TVPA set a standard for countries around the world to strengthen efforts to prosecute traffickers, increase protection for foreign national trafficking victims, and expand related foreign assistance programs. By 2021, Congress reauthorized the TVPA five times with expanded requirements to strengthen U.S. government action (see appendix 2 also for a timeline and summary of the TVPA reauthorizations).

Implementation of the TVPA has been a bipartisan issue. In 2002, the Bush administration built on the passage of the TVPA during the Clinton administration by establishing the President's Interagency Task Force to Monitor and Combat Trafficking in Persons.[78] In 2012, the Obama administration issued an executive order to combat trafficking in federal contracts and in 2016 produced a National Intelligence Estimate on global human trafficking.[79] In 2020, the Trump administration launched the United States' first National Action Plan to Combat Human Trafficking.[80] Many U.S. government agencies participate in the President's Interagency Task Force to Monitor and Combat Trafficking in Persons, including the Departments of Defense, Health and Human Services (HHS), Homeland Security (DHS), Justice, Labor, State, and Treasury, and the U.S. Agency for International Development (USAID). The State Department uses its annual TIP report to encourage like-minded governments to enact trafficking laws and improve their implementation.[81] The Obama administration added the United States to its TIP report rankings, reviewing the nation's progress in combating trafficking domestically using the same framework the United States applies to other countries. Other agencies have standalone strategies to fight human trafficking: for example, the Department of Homeland Security issued its first plan in 2020, and USAID—considered a leader among international development agencies in combating human trafficking—recently updated its 2012 policy, releasing a revised version in January 2021 at the end of the Trump administration.

The Department of Labor contributes research and reporting that exposes labor abuses around the world, including by maintaining a list of goods (and their source countries) that it suspects were produced with the use of child or forced labor. As of 2020, the Labor Department listed 155 goods from 77 countries. Recently, the department expanded the list to include any goods created "with inputs that are produced with forced labor or child labor"—which will capture broader situations of abuse in response to a new congressional mandate.[82]

In addition, the U.S. government has a range of financial tools to combat the industry's illicit profits, including sanctions authorities to freeze traffickers' assets and legal requirements that financial institutions report suspicious activity. The Treasury Department issued guidelines to assist the financial sector in detecting the range of money laundering tactics that human traffickers and their facilitators employ to conceal their profits, avoid detection, and expand their criminal networks.[83] Those guidelines build on similar global efforts by the Financial Action Task Force and the Liechtenstein Initiative for Finance Against Slavery and Trafficking.[84]

Congress continues to combat human trafficking through additional legislation, appropriations, and oversight efforts. For example, it has taken steps to address labor trafficking and forced labor—from a specific forced labor statute in 2000 (18 USC §1589) to provisions in the 2010 Dodd-Frank Act that require responsible minerals sourcing. In 2018, Congress took the critical step of holding websites that host sex-trafficking ads accountable through the Allow States and Victims to Fight Online Sex Trafficking Act. In the 2021 National Defense Authorization Act, Congress also required all companies registered in the United States to disclose their actual owners, closing a loophole that permitted traffickers, terrorists, and other criminals to cloak themselves in shell companies.[85]

U.S. government efforts to combat forced labor and trafficking have been bolstered by the global movement for responsible business conduct. In 2011, the United Nations issued its Guiding Principles on Business and Human Rights, laying out a global standard for how corporations should respect human rights—including labor rights. In 2014, governments, employers, and workers voted to adopt a protocol to supplement the 1930 Forced Labour Convention, requiring government action to end the practice, including developing national action plans and providing victims with protection and compensation.[86] Some governments—including Australia, the United Kingdom, and the state of California—have required large corporations to report on their actions to prevent forced labor across their supply chains; however, transparency-only requirements are producing too little change.[87] Notably, laws in France, Germany, and the Netherlands (which, in the Netherlands' case, focused on child labor) go further in requiring that companies take due diligence measures to assess potential human rights abuses related to their business activities and offer remedies.[88] Building on these examples, negotiations are underway to develop more stringent global standards for responsible business conduct, including a European Union–wide mandatory human rights due diligence law and a legally binding UN treaty on business and human rights, which, if enacted, would help address this critical gap.[89]

In addition, institutional investors, including mutual and equity funds, are encouraging greater private-sector attention to forced labor and human trafficking by ensuring the associated social costs are appropriately priced into business models through environmental, social, and governance (ESG) frameworks. Such efforts recognize the financial implications that forced labor and human trafficking pose, for example, through reputational threats, earnings volatility, and supply chain disruption.

SHORTCOMINGS

Although the Palermo Protocol has been widely adopted globally, implementation has been weak. Of the 188 assessed governments in the State Department's annual TIP report, most rank below Tier 1, which is the only tier in which countries meet the minimum U.S. government standards for the elimination of human trafficking (see figure 4).[90] Broadly, Tier 2 countries' governments do not yet meet minimum U.S. government standards but are "making significant efforts" to do so, while Tier 2 watch-list countries—despite significant or increasing numbers of victims of severe forms of human trafficking—have not increased efforts to address those numbers. Tier 3 countries are neither meeting minimum standards nor taking meaningful action to do so.[91]

The U.S. government's own efforts have also fallen short: twenty years after the passage of the TVPA, the U.S. government is still missing critical opportunities to better leverage U.S. tools and capacities to combat modern slavery. Its current framework is undermined by insufficient authorities, weak accountability, limited investment, and inadequate data.

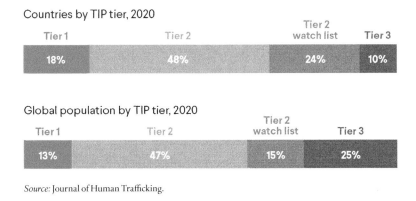

Figure 4. MOST GOVERNMENTS DO NOT MEET MINI-
MUM STANDARDS FOR ADDRESSING TRAFFICKING

Countries by TIP tier, 2020

Tier 1	Tier 2	Tier 2 watch list	Tier 3
18%	48%	24%	10%

Global population by TIP tier, 2020

Tier 1	Tier 2	Tier 2 watch list	Tier 3
13%	47%	15%	25%

Source: Journal of Human Trafficking.

Insufficient Institutional Authorities and Coordination

The United States lacks sufficient authorities and coordination across the federal government to address human trafficking adequately, instead treating this issue as ancillary to broader foreign policy concerns. The U.S. government pays too little attention to how human trafficking undermines economic growth, fuels conflict and instability, and threatens democracy and sustainable development.[92] Coordination is minimal between officials across the human rights, national security, economic, labor, and development sectors, as is investment in human trafficking outside trafficking-focused offices. The intelligence community has promised to address human trafficking, pledging in October 2020 to produce a U.S. assessment; however, this report risks being overlooked as an isolated product, as was the case with the 2016 National Intelligence Estimate on global human trafficking.

Despite the potential pool of $150 billion in trafficking-related illicit profits to track and seize, the Treasury Department has listed human trafficking in only a few of its economic sanctions determinations, due in part to insufficient prioritization of this approach.[93] Government officials fail to investigate many of the financial sector's reports on suspicious activity, and law enforcement, focused on criminal charges, pays insufficient attention to civil and administrative authorities to disrupt trafficking—including the illicit use of the financial system. The combined result is that relatively few trafficking profits are seized.[94]

Domestically, the Trump administration's restrictive immigration policies left migrants more vulnerable to human trafficking, and its anti-immigrant rhetoric and policies discouraged survivors from cooperating with law enforcement to hold traffickers accountable. Those policies build on a history of exploitative labor recruitment systems—including through guest-worker programs from the United States to Qatar and around the world—that contribute to the trafficking of millions of migrant workers and place tens of millions more at risk (see appendix 1 for an analysis of labor exploitation in the Arabian Gulf).[95] In the United States, inconsistent rules and requirements across visa programs—H-1B, H-2, G-5, the J-1 exchange program, and others—as well as weak enforcement of existing regulations foster abuse and human trafficking by recruiters and employers.

Procurement systems also risk enabling labor trafficking. The U.S. government is one of the world's largest purchasers of consumer goods and spent an estimated $600 billion in fiscal year 2020 on civilian and defense contracts, yet it does not monitor the behavior of suppliers and subcontractors across much of its global supply chain.[96] This area needs reform: for example, as recently as 2019, the Defense Department was implicated in labor trafficking when U.S. government inspectors uncovered forced labor perpetrated by Defense Department contractors on U.S. bases in Kuwait; similar violations were reported in 2005 on U.S. bases in Iraq.[97]

Despite USAID's commitments to preventing human trafficking, its policies remain too limited in scope and fail to address human trafficking as a critical challenge to sustainable development.[98] Furthermore, although the Sustainable Development Goals (SDGs) include three related targets and governments have joined forces through such initiatives as the 2017 Call to Action to End Forced Labor, Modern Slavery and Human Trafficking and the Alliance 8.7 initiative (a reference to the SDG target 8.7 on human trafficking), meaningful coordination is limited, and anti-trafficking measures remain siloed from the broader sustainable development community.[99] In addition, U.S. anti-trafficking efforts pay limited attention to forced marriage or organ removal, neither of which is covered in detail in either the State Department's annual TIP report or the Labor Department's work on child exploitation, or invested in through anti-trafficking programs.

Weak Accountability

Despite a law enforcement focus on combating human trafficking, impunity remains the norm—for individual traffickers, corporations, criminal and terrorist networks, and governments. Fewer than twelve thousand of the estimated twenty-five million cases of human trafficking were prosecuted in 2019, and among those, detected labor trafficking cases were less likely to be prosecuted or reach convictions than sex-trafficking cases.[100] Similarly, in the United States, federal prosecutors brought a mere 220 federal criminal trafficking cases in 2019, of which only twelve were for forced labor.[101] Where law enforcement is effective, research shows that exploitation can be reduced: in Cambodia and the Philippines, for example, increased investigation and prosecution of perpetrators facilitated a drop in child trafficking for sexual exploitation in commercial establishments.[102]

Greater accountability is needed to ensure slavery-free supply chains that respect workers' rights and protect multinational companies from regulatory and reputational risk. Recognizing the Department of Homeland Security's Customs and Border Protection (CBP)'s failure to enforce the 1930 Tariff Act, Congress closed a loophole in 2016, in order to require CBP to block the import of goods into the U.S. market that it suspects were produced with forced labor. If implemented as intended, the law now has the potential to incentivize multinational corporations to prevent forced labor in their supply chains or risk suspended shipments and unfavorable press should CBP detain their goods at the border. CBP's tools would be more effective, however, if better integrated in a coordinated government response and better staffed with a limited number of additional personnel at headquarters and in ports to fully implement the law—requiring an additional $5 million for human resources.[103]

Executive action has also undercut corporate accountability: for example, in a 2020 Supreme Court case on child forced labor in the cocoa industry, the Trump administration undermined its anti-trafficking commitments by arguing that employers should be shielded from liability for child slavery in their overseas supply chains (the court has not yet ruled on the case).[104] Furthermore, accountability efforts have too often overlooked the priorities of the survivors themselves, including by failing to ensure victim restitution and by providing only temporary assistance without job training that leaves survivors at risk of falling prey again to traffickers.

Essential to eradicating forced labor from the private sector is the complicated task of knowing where suppliers operate and how they manage human trafficking risks. A wide range of technology tools—including some funded by the U.S. government—offer new and innovative ways to support these efforts, which include helping multinational corporations and employers protect their workers, improve their visibility across their supply chains, and increase their compliance with anti-trafficking laws. For instance, artificial intelligence and machine learning could allow governments and multinationals to predict forced labor risks across an entire supply chain, enabling them to prioritize ethical suppliers; a new decision support tool, for example—developed by the Global Fund to End Modern Slavery and to be released open source—has 84 percent accuracy in identifying forced labor risks.

Limited Resources

Reforming exploitative systems to protect the worst off—those held in slavery-like conditions—offers broad societal benefits. Despite the projected return on investment, human trafficking is too often regarded as a niche issue rather than a metric of economic health, protection of labor rights, and respect for the rule of law—and anti-trafficking efforts are persistently under-resourced by governments, philanthropy, and the private sector.

The U.S. government and its partners cannot end human trafficking with the funding currently available. Between 2000 and 2017, Organization for Economic Cooperation and Development (OECD) donor countries dedicated an average of only $12 per trafficking victim each year.[105] Of this Official Development Assistance (ODA), the United States was the largest single contributor, providing 42.8 percent of the declared bilateral ODA resources from 2000 to 2017 through USAID, the State Department, and other agencies.[106] However, given the scale and breadth of human trafficking globally and its implications for U.S. foreign policy interests, the investment in efforts to combat it remains paltry.

Inadequate Data and Evidence

Anti-trafficking efforts are undermined by an absence of data on the prevalence of human trafficking, the determinants of exploitation, and the effectiveness of program interventions from the community level to global supply chains. Despite the $150 billion in illicit profits associated with human trafficking, governments, corporations, and organizations invest too little to produce the prevalence estimates needed to better understand the scale of this hidden crime and do not conduct rigorous program evaluations to determine what measures work best to combat human trafficking. As a consequence, anti-trafficking actors are limited by the available information about detected victims and cases, which understates the scope of human trafficking, and without rigorous evaluations they continue to invest in untested interventions. Furthermore, civil society organizations on the front lines of anti-trafficking efforts lack the capacity and resources to collect and analyze data. Information gaps are further exacerbated by a lack of coordination between organizations to standardize and synthesize human trafficking data into a comprehensive picture.[107]

RECOMMENDATIONS

To address these gaps, the U.S. government and other governments worldwide should enact reforms that improve efforts to combat human trafficking. They should strengthen institutional authorities and coordination; improve accountability for individuals, networks, and businesses; invest sufficient resources to reduce vulnerability to trafficking and support comprehensive services for survivors; and prioritize data-gathering and evaluation to make policies and programs more effective. This agenda can be accomplished with modest investment of time and funding and promises significant returns for U.S. economic and security interests.

STRENGTHEN INSTITUTIONAL AUTHORITIES AND COORDINATION

To end human trafficking, the U.S. government should enact structural reforms to improve institutional efforts to combat the crime. It should strengthen the U.S. national action plan to halt human trafficking; institute procurement reform; update immigration law to deter the exploitation of migrant workers; amplify anti-trafficking measures from the national security and intelligence communities; strengthen the sustainable development efforts to combat trafficking; and evaluate U.S. policies on overlooked forms of human trafficking.

Expand the U.S. National Action Plan to Combat Human Trafficking

The White House—together with the Defense, Homeland Security, Justice, State, and Treasury Departments; USAID; the intelligence community; the U.S. Securities and Exchange Commission (SEC); and the U.S. Trade Representative—should issue an executive order and release an updated National Action Plan to Combat Human Trafficking, building on the strategy issued by the Trump administration in October 2020 but expanding its global focus. The executive order and national action plan should

- articulate a coordinated approach to preventing forced labor that aligns U.S. government efforts across global supply chains;

- identify a comprehensive accountability strategy that applies the full range of criminal, civil, administrative, and collection authorities to disrupt trafficking and forced labor, recognizing that tools beyond criminal prosecution receive too little attention;

- delegate the president's authority granted in the TVPA (2000) to the State and Treasury Departments to establish a sanctions program dedicated to combating human trafficking and expressly linked with the broader Global Magnitsky human rights and anti-corruption sanctions program (with at least $500,000 dedicated annually to investigations, either through congressional appropriations or the president's budget);

- improve data sharing, referrals, and coordination between law enforcement and intelligence officials to help financial-sector actors pursue financial accountability, starting with a strategic analysis of financial institutions' suspicious activity reports that identifies trends and analyzes how human traffickers intersect with U.S. financial institutions;

- reform the Trump administration's immigration-related commitments in the first national action plan to better address the relationship between human trafficking and migration while encouraging trafficking survivors in the United States to seek help without fear of deportation; and

- strengthen the humanitarian community's response—including UN agencies and nongovernmental organizations—to address human trafficking as a protection priority for refugees and internally displaced people, including by conducting risk analyses, incorporating anti-trafficking efforts in humanitarian activities, and coordinating with anti-trafficking partners.

Enact Immigration Reform to Combat the Exploitation of Migrant Workers

Recognizing that exploitative labor recruitment systems—in the United States and around the world—contribute to the trafficking of migrant workers, the U.S. government should combat human trafficking domestically and lead by example by reforming its own temporary work-visa system, under which hundreds of thousands of workers are recruited to the United States.

To this end, the U.S. government should increase the safety, transparency, and efficiency of labor recruitment systems that are currently plagued by outdated technologies, informal operators, and widespread corruption. Such reforms will help prevent human trafficking in product supply chains, including debt bondage fueled by worker-paid fees from exploitative brokers.[108] Specifically, the U.S. government should

- align the currently inconsistent rules and requirements across visa programs—H-1B, H-2, G-5, the J-1 exchange program, and others—and increase enforcement of existing regulations, to prevent abuse and human trafficking by recruiters and employers;

- modify its sponsorship system so that workers' legal status is not tied to their employer, which can force workers to stay in exploitative situations or risk deportation; hold recruiters and employers liable for recruitment abuses; prohibit recruitment fees paid by workers; and increase worker access to legal aid and information, as recommended by the Migration that Works coalition;

- regulate and monitor labor recruitment agencies both within U.S. territories and for U.S. government contracts overseas; and

- extend labor rights protections, including occupational safety and health standards, to migrant laborers—including children.[109]

As part of congressional efforts to address the discriminatory immigration laws that further increase the vulnerability of migrant workers to trafficking and other abuses, the U.S. government should

- triple the ten thousand U-visas cap and correct the unacceptable delay in T-visa processing;

- restore asylum eligibility for domestic violence survivors, which was rescinded by the Trump administration;

- include a path to citizenship and workplace protections for agricultural workers on U.S. farms such as through the proposed Fairness for Farmworkers Act; and

- ensure federal workplace protections for domestic workers as proposed in the Domestic Workers' Bill of Rights.[110]

In parallel to its domestic efforts, the U.S. government should encourage partner nations to regulate recruitment agencies and brokers, conduct regular oversight of recruitment systems, hold recruiters and employers liable for abuses, and encourage companies to cover recruitment costs and use ethical recruitment agencies in line with recommendations by the ILO, the International Organization for Migration, and the former Special Rapporteur on Trafficking in Persons Maria Grazia Giammarinaro.[111]

Enact Procurement Reform to Prevent Human Trafficking

The U.S. government should address the risk of human trafficking and forced labor in its contracts, grants, investments, and loans. To strengthen the government's compliance and improve procurement processes, Congress should

- request a Government Accountability Office review of agency efforts to prevent human trafficking in federal contracts, which should assess current acquisition processes, evaluating how the riskiest contracts are identified, examining protocols for on-the-ground audits, and comparing government contracts with proposed model language to protect human rights across supply chains;

- explore legislative steps to address the review's findings and conduct regular oversight of the executive branch's efforts, including through hearings; and

- require Defense Department reporting on the number of contracts that include anti-trafficking clauses, as mandated in 2018 for the Department of State, USAID, the Department of Labor, and the Office of Management and Budget.[112]

To address gaps in procurement oversight, U.S. government agencies with higher spending and greater risk of human trafficking in their contracts—including the Defense, Homeland Security, and State Departments, and USAID—should

- designate full-time senior officials responsible for overseeing anti-trafficking acquisition rules, as promised in the Trump administration's National Action Plan to Combat Human Trafficking;

- incentivize contractors to use technology to host worker outreach initiatives, creating channels for workers to report grievances; and

- encourage similar procurement reform by bilateral governments and multilateral institutions, from the United Nations to the Organization for Security and Cooperation in Europe (OSCE).

Amplify National Security and Intelligence Community Efforts to Combat Trafficking

To better address the security implications of human trafficking, the U.S. government should

- revise the 2011 U.S. Strategy to Combat Transnational Organized Crime to address human trafficking by criminal enterprises as a strategic and fundraising tool;

- complete an intelligence assessment of human trafficking with a nexus to the United States, as promised in the U.S. National Action Plan to Combat Human Trafficking, and use its findings to inform an agenda for intelligence products on specific human trafficking issues;

- appoint a national intelligence officer for human rights to lead analysis on the economic and security implications of human trafficking, which should include attention to official corruption and state complicity and address how criminal networks and terrorist groups exploit migrant and smuggling routes; and

- encourage increased attention by the UN Security Council to the security implications of human trafficking, including through additional targeted sanctions.

Strengthen Sustainable Development Efforts
to Combat Human Trafficking

The global development community does not address the threat of trafficking to its broader priorities, including democracy, good governance, economic growth, and poverty alleviation. To rectify this gap, the U.S. government should

- strengthen the 2021 USAID policy on countering trafficking in persons to improve procurement regulations, require trafficking mitigation and risk assessments across USAID programs to ensure that they do not increase vulnerabilities to human trafficking, and improve coordination between USAID missions and U.S. embassies in origin and destination countries in cases of transnational trafficking;

- host a donor dialogue in 2021 to identify opportunities—in the context of COVID-19 recovery and beyond—to promote economic reforms that help prevent modern slavery, including policies that emphasize human capital formation, increase social safety nets, protect labor rights, and extend financial inclusion;

- identify opportunities to combat trafficking in the context of the Sustainable Development Goals—including in the upcoming high-level political forum—and encourage multilateral development banks to pay greater attention to the development implications of human trafficking; and

- ensure the Biden administration's promised summit for democracy includes a focus on human trafficking, given the relationship between anti-trafficking efforts, corruption, and good governance.[113]

Evaluate U.S. Policies on Overlooked Forms of Human Trafficking

Recognizing that its efforts to combat human trafficking currently do too little to address trafficking in persons for forced marriage and for organ removal, the State Department should take the following steps.

- Together with the Labor Department and USAID, the State Department should establish a working group of experts from the forced marriage, forced labor, and human trafficking communities, including victims of forced marriage, to build alignment with recent steps by some civil society and multilateral organizations—including the ILO—to explore whether forced marriage should be recognized as a form of modern slavery, human trafficking, and forced labor. The working group should propose ways in which the anti-trafficking community can best intervene to support ongoing efforts to prevent and address forced marriage.

• The State Department should also draft a report analyzing exploitation for organ removal and identifying responses, as called for in H.R. 7805, the Stop Predatory Organ Trafficking Act of 2020.[114] Based on this assessment, the department should coordinate with relevant agencies to develop a targeted response plan—including steps to seize illicit assets.

IMPROVE ACCOUNTABILITY

To promote accountability, the U.S. government should strengthen corporate responsibility for forced labor in supply chains; prohibit trade of goods made with forced labor; increase trafficking prosecution; strengthen cybercrime-fighting strategies to address sex trafficking; and improve accountability for survivors.

Strengthen Corporate Responsibility for Forced Labor in Supply Chains

U.S. policies and laws should encourage firms to change their purchasing and financing practices to eliminate exploitative practices and remedy existing harm, and they should underscore that companies are responsible for addressing human rights harms, including forced labor and human trafficking, related to their suppliers' conduct. To this end, the following four steps should be prioritized.

• Congress should pass a law mandating strong and effective human rights due diligence arrangements for corporations. To avoid regulatory fragmentation, these should be consistent with the emerging global human rights due diligence regimes, such as in Europe. They should also build on existing U.S. policies—for example, the commitments already made in the 2016 U.S. National Action Plan on Responsible Business Conduct and the success of the U.S. Foreign Corrupt

Practices Act of 1977 in incentivizing companies to invest in compliance regimes, provide training, and change corporate culture.[115] A new law should prohibit companies from purchasing goods and services implicated in forced labor; require due diligence reporting; and authorize the Justice Department and the SEC to investigate allegations, impose fines, and charge violations. The law should appoint the SEC to the U.S. government's anti-trafficking bodies and create an SEC position to oversee implementation.

- The Justice Department should argue in support of corporate accountability when allegations are made against multinational companies due to forced labor in their supply chains. The Trump administration did not do so, including in the pending 2020 Supreme Court case *Nestlé USA, Inc. v. Doe I*; the Biden administration should correct this position by withdrawing the brief submitted by the solicitor general and suggesting that the court not rely on the government's oral argument.

- The SEC should strengthen ESG regulations in financial markets, including labor rights protections and forced labor prevention. The SEC should encourage institutional investors, including mutual and equity funds, to explicitly include metrics related to human trafficking and ethical supply chain management in their ESG criteria and disclosures, such as those focused on human capital. Recognizing that ESG practices correspond with stronger financial returns, the SEC should also encourage investors to back companies that address forced labor risk in their supply chains.[116] Furthermore, the SEC should enhance shareholder engagement in ESG processes to accelerate progress toward increased corporate accountability.

Prohibit Trade of Goods Made with Forced Labor

Recognizing that trade and customs policies at home and abroad offer another critical tool to help end human trafficking, the U.S. government should implement the following strategies.

- At the WTO conference scheduled for late 2021, the United States should lead WTO members and observers in adopting a ministerial declaration on preventing forced labor in the production of goods that would both articulate a roadmap toward a formal WTO committee on trade, human trafficking, and forced labor and strengthen coordination between the WTO and ILO.

- The United States should fully implement domestically Section 307 of the 1930 Tariff Act, which authorizes CBP to block goods produced by forced labor from entering U.S. markets—providing a powerful accountability tool. To do so, CBP should expand the investigation and enforcement of withhold release orders and establish a more transparent process for investigations, findings, and remediation plans, which would benefit businesses and advocates alike.[117] To improve investigative capacity, DHS should identify resource requirements across CBP—from the Forced Labor Division to ports—and set performance indicators related to forced labor enforcement as recommended by the Government Accountability Office in October 2020.[118]

- The United States should encourage other countries to adopt similar customs laws to prohibit goods produced with forced labor from entering their national markets, as Canada and Mexico did in the United States-Mexico-Canada Agreement (USMCA)—for example, by encouraging the Group of Seven and the Group of Twenty to pursue related commitments. Drawing on the USMCA model, the U.S. Trade Representative should incorporate anti-trafficking provisions in future U.S. trade agreements.

- The United States should also use U.S. trade preference programs—intended to foster economic growth in developing countries—to encourage stronger protections for labor rights and prevention of human trafficking and forced labor. The Women's Economic Empowerment in Trade Act pending in the U.S. Senate would accomplish this goal, promoting U.S. values while strengthening the global economy.[119]

Increase Trafficking Prosecution

The Biden administration should increase trafficking-related prosecution within the United States and globally, paying targeted attention to labor trafficking violations, which are underrepresented. The U.S. government should

- scale nationally the U.S. anti-trafficking coordination teams that link officials within HHS, DHS, the Justice Department, the Department of Labor, and the FBI and that have been remarkably effective in increasing trafficking prosecutions—charges and convictions rose by 75 and

106 percent in districts with coordination teams relative to 7 and 28 percent in districts without;

- support in other nations around the world the replication and testing of its prosecution coordination teams through rule-of-law support;

- set targets and track progress to improve the rate of prosecution and conviction for forced labor, train police and prosecutors to pursue labor trafficking cases, and protect workers from retaliation when they report cases;

- address forced labor perpetrated by the diplomatic community in the United States by fully implementing existing laws; and

- use its extraterritorial jurisdiction granted under 18 U.S.C. 1596 to pursue justice for trafficking victims held in forced labor in global supply chains.[120]

Strengthen Cybercrime-Fighting Strategies to Address Sex Trafficking

In the twenty-first century, the crime of sex trafficking has migrated to online—and sometimes hidden—platforms. To address it, tech companies and law enforcement authorities should

- amplify efforts to combat online sexual exploitation, including using technology to disrupt trafficking networks, surface suspicious financial behavior, identify minors, and develop innovative tools to aid online victims;

- shift from episodic sting operations to routine approaches; and

- prioritize better data collection to understand how online networks facilitate trafficking and other forms of sexual exploitation.

Promote Accountability for Survivors

Accountability for human trafficking should be defined as justice for survivors—not just as prosecution of traffickers—and victim remediation and compensation should be prioritized. To support survivors' recovery, the U.S. government should

- provide multiyear assistance for survivors including housing, job training, and mental health services;

- encourage businesses implicated in forced labor to provide effective remedies for survivors;

- reform U- and T-visa programs to provide all trafficking survivors with access to visas and social services, regardless of their participation in criminal cases against perpetrators (until it institutes this assistance, the U.S. government should use "continued presence," a provisional form of immigration relief, to protect victims who could be potential witnesses);

- increase the seizure of trafficker assets to compensate victims by training prosecutors on forfeiture in human trafficking cases, ensuring that restitution ordered in criminal cases is remitted to victim-witnesses, and supporting survivors in pursuing civil remedies;

- encourage all U.S. states to pass safe harbor laws that protect trafficking survivors from arrest and prosecution for crimes that traffickers force them to commit, pass a federal criminal *vacatur* statute to allow all such convictions to be removed from trafficking victims' records, and advocate that other governments pursue the same approach; and

- encourage other nations to implement the Palermo Protocol and national anti-trafficking laws in a manner that emphasizes survivors' rights and the systemic nature of exploitation, shifting from a law enforcement approach to one that prioritizes protecting labor rights, including the freedom of association—because workers who are able to collectively organize are less vulnerable to forced labor.[121]

INCREASE RESOURCES

To correct for dramatic under-resourcing in the field, all donors, including the United States, should step up their investment through strategic and coordinated anti-trafficking measures.

Expand Funding to Counter Human Trafficking

The U.S. government should increase resources for combating human trafficking by pursuing these investments:

- appropriate, via Congress, $1 billion for combating human trafficking in the United States and around the world, as recommended by the Alliance to End Slavery and Trafficking—expanding Congress's FY 2021 enactment of $620 million, and providing critical resources to address the additional economic and health challenges that trafficking survivors and those at risk face due to the COVID-19 pandemic;

- launch, via USAID, a Grand Challenge to Prevent Modern Slavery, leveraging an established model to mobilize governments, companies, and foundations to develop new ways to address long-standing development challenges; and

- encourage the multilateral development banks to integrate human trafficking reduction across their lending and policy advice to governments to better address the development implications of human trafficking.[122]

Invest in Technology to Identify Forced Labor

The U.S. government should invest in developing technological tools to identify forced labor and encourage corporations and multilateral partners to do the same.[123] For example, to aid Tariff Act enforcement, CBP should assess the potential for technology—including product DNA tracing, artificial intelligence, and machine learning—to identify imported goods produced using forced labor.[124]

To glean information from workers about human trafficking risks, Congress should encourage the private sector—such as through a due diligence law—to leverage mobile technology to hear directly from workers, enabling them to report grievances and to hold businesses— and, where appropriate, direct managers—accountable for their workplace treatment.

EXPAND DATA AND EVIDENCE

Anti-trafficking actors should prioritize data production on the prevalence of human trafficking and analysis of the efficacy of measures to combat this crime.

Close the Trafficking Data Gap

The U.S. government should join other governments, foundations, civil society organizations, and corporations in launching a joint initiative on human trafficking that increases the investment in and coordination of trafficking data, evaluation, and learning. The initiative should foster collaboration across transnational trafficking corridors and supply chains to strengthen intelligence about human trafficking risks and coordinate responses.[125] To increase the available data, partners should prioritize capacity-building for civil society organizations to strengthen information collection, including through survivor case management systems, and expand the reach of data collection efforts through remote technology. In parallel, the U.S. government and its partners should commit to higher evidentiary standards for bilateral investments, incentivizing greater attention to rigorous quantitative and qualitative data in the human trafficking field. Expanded data and evidence will inform more effective action at the scale necessary for genuine progress in the fight to end human trafficking.

CONCLUSION

Human trafficking is more than a violation of human rights: it is also a threat to national security, economic growth, and sustainable development. Critics who challenge the allocation of political and financial capital to combat human trafficking underestimate trafficking's role in bolstering abusive regimes and criminal, terrorist, and armed groups; weakening global supply chains; fueling corruption; and undermining good governance. Human trafficking can be eradicated with a comprehensive and coordinated response, advancing U.S. economic and security interests by blocking the $150 billion in illicit profits for traffickers, boosting GDP with improved productivity and human capital, and saving governments the direct costs of assisting survivors.

To win the fight against human trafficking, the United States and its partners should build on the Palermo Protocol's legal frameworks and related national legislation—including the U.S. Trafficking Victims Protection Act—with a twenty-first-century approach. This approach should involve leaders across government, the private sector, multilateral institutions, and civil society to strengthen institutional authorities and coordination, improve accountability, increase resources, and expand evidence and data.

APPENDIX 1

Human trafficking in all of its manifestations remains an endemic problem in every region of the world. Pressing challenges that demand greater U.S. and international attention include the targeting of Uyghur Muslims for forced labor in Chinese reeducation camps; the victimization of Latin American migrants via debt bondage at the U.S. border; the subjection of domestic laborers to abuse under the *kafala* framework employed across the Arabian Gulf; the exploitation of children by traffickers in a booming sex tourism business in Brazil; and the enslavement of young girls trapped in forced marriages in India, home to the largest number of child brides in the world.

CASE STUDIES

China

Forced labor is a grave problem in China. According to the 2020 U.S. Trafficking in Persons Report, both Chinese nationals and foreigners are targeted.[126] The labor is common in cities, where internal migrants from rural areas are exploited for it.[127] In 2020, the U.S. Department of Labor's list of goods produced with child or forced labor added six new goods sourced from China—five produced using state-sponsored forced labor.[128]

Indeed, in China, forced labor has been perpetrated not only by traffickers but also as government policy. Beginning in the mid-1950s, the Chinese Communist Party began a reeducation through labor (RTL), or *laojiao*, program aimed at political dissidents, unofficial religious groups, those suspected of minor offenses, and others.[129] This program was extrajudicial, meaning that people were sent to labor camps without trial or conviction. In 2007, an estimated four hundred thousand people toiled in Chinese RTL camps. In 2013, following an international pressure campaign, the government officially abolished them, prompting the U.S. government to move China up a tier in its Trafficking in Persons Report ranking.[130]

However, the RTL program's legacy continues through so-called detention facilities in which prisoners are compelled either to undergo reeducation or to work in conditions that amount to forced labor.[131] In recent years, this practice has intersected with a brutal campaign against Uyghur Muslims. Between 2017 and 2019, at least eighty thousand Uyghurs and other marginalized minorities were transported from Xinjiang, a western province, to various areas across China, where they have been subjected to forced labor; more than one million have been detained for reeducation.[132] Several high-profile multinational corporations—among them H&M, Kraft, Coca-Cola, and Gap—have been alleged to use suppliers that rely on the forced labor of Uyghurs.[133] The situation implicates the textile and apparels sector in particular, given that 20 percent of all cotton sold globally comes from the Xinjiang region, though companies have cited a lack of visibility in their supply chains as an obstacle to ensuring that their goods are slavery free.[134]

In response to the Chinese government's exploitation of its Uyghur minority population, in 2020, the U.S. Customs and Border Protection (CBP) issued eight withhold release orders against goods made by Chinese companies and manufacturers.[135] In January 2021, CBP issued a region-wide withhold release order against cotton and tomatoes from the Xinjiang region, a decision human rights groups had long advocated.[136] Congress has also taken action, enacting in 2020 the Uyghur Human Rights Policy Act, which calls on the U.S. government to issue sanctions against implicated Chinese officials and report to Congress on progress in addressing these human rights abuses.[137] In 2021, Congress reintroduced the Uyghur Forced Labor Prevention Act, which would prohibit importation of goods from Xinjiang produced with forced labor and would require U.S. public companies to disclose their involvement with the region.

United States

The debate over illegal immigration into the United States features widespread concern about the risks of human trafficking and human smuggling, which can affect migrant workers who voluntarily enter into a smuggling arrangement and then fall prey to debt bondage and trafficking, particularly when an existing arrangement turns out to be fraudulent.[138]

During the Trump administration, the U.S. government implemented several harsh immigration measures that increased the vulnerability of migrants to traffickers. Chief among these was a new policy that undermined the T visa, a creation of the 2000 Trafficking Victims Protection Act that sought to encourage human trafficking victims to come forward by providing legal status. The T-visa program allows undocumented human trafficking victims to remain in the United States with work authorization. They are able to reunite with family members and have a path to become lawful permanent residents and, eventually, citizens.[139] The number of T visas granted plummeted during the Trump era, with those denied then referred to immigration court for deportation proceedings, reducing the number of victims who came forward and decreasing the likelihood that traffickers would be held accountable.[140] Similarly, the Trump administration also undercut the U-visa program, which provides legal status to noncitizen victims of a range of crimes, including trafficking; in 2018, the administration executed a new policy that permitted the deportation of those waiting for their claims to be processed, discouraging trafficking victims from reporting their traffickers and contributing to a decline in the number of visa applicants.[141] For both the T- and U-visa programs, processing delays and deportation threats undermined the safety these visas were intended to provide and contributed to situations that make survivors vulnerable to revictimization.[142]

The Biden administration should restore and strengthen immigration protections for human trafficking survivors, including by removing the requirement that survivors cooperate with criminal investigations to be eligible for T and U visas. Protecting migrants from exploitation also will require comprehensive immigration reform to stem the tide of those desperate to enter the United States in the first instance. As part of that reform, U.S. immigration processes should include screening procedures to assess whether migrants are victims of forced labor, sex trafficking, or other forms of modern slavery.

The Arabian Gulf

Across the Gulf region, many Arab nations practice the *kafala* (sponsorship) system, a framework that ties migrants' legal status to their employers and creates a situation primed for abuse.[143] Although many migrants voluntarily come to the region looking to earn money for their families at home, in practice, labor under the *kafala* system can be tantamount to slavery. Historically, few (if any) legal protections for migrant workers and little oversight of employers have been in place or practiced. Particularly exploitative aspects include the common practice of seizing migrant workers' passports, the requirement that migrant workers get permission from employers before leaving their jobs, and the threat of arrest if a migrant worker flees an abusive employer.[144]

Migrants laboring in domestic work—who are disproportionately female—are particularly vulnerable to abuses under the *kafala* system. By living in an employer's home, workers are unprotected against restrictions on their access to food, shelter, and freedom of movement.[145] Many migrant domestic workers whose passports have been seized are forced to work long hours, have their pay deducted or withheld, and in some instances are subject to physical, sexual, and verbal abuse.[146]

Several nations have begun to reform the system, a promising trend toward abolition of the practice. After years of pressure, in 2017 the Qatari government signed an agreement with the International Labor Organization (ILO) to improve its labor practices in advance of the 2022 International Federation of Association Football World Cup; in 2020, the government passed laws allowing migrant workers to leave their employers before the terms of the contract have expired, becoming the first country that practices the *kafala* system to do so and the second in the region after Kuwait to give migrant workers a minimum wage. These reforms, if fully implemented, would go a long way toward abolishing the system.[147]

Likewise, in 2020 the Saudi government pledged several changes to ease its *kafala* system, including allowing migrant workers to switch jobs and leave the country without an employer's consent, maintaining digital records of migrant workers' contracts, and enabling migrant workers to apply to the government for social services. Nevertheless, many gaps in the system remain, leaving migrant workers at risk.[148] As advocates in Gulf nations continue to press for reform, the United States and other like-minded countries have a critical role to play in employing diplomatic tools to pressure for wholesale reform and the abolition of all forced labor.

Brazil

Sexual exploitation of children in the context of travel and tourism is an endemic issue in Brazil, with tourists primarily from Europe and the United States traveling to resort and coastal areas where the prevalence of commercial sexual exploitation of children is high.[149] The age of consent in Brazil is only fourteen. Afro-Brazilian children facing racism and the legacy of slavery are more likely to be impoverished and therefore vulnerable to sexual exploitation, and persistent corruption among law enforcement undermines community trust, inhibiting access to justice for victims.[150]

Although Brazil reformed its penal code in 2016 to comply with the Palermo Protocol, underenforcement persists.[151] In addition, the country lacks specialized shelters for survivors of sex trafficking, including children.[152] Brazil's child protection system does feature guardianship councils to help connect children with critical social services, but these mechanisms are underfunded and cannot guarantee privacy to minors, which undermines their efficacy both for child survivors and children at risk of exploitation.[153]

The tourism industry has taken steps to combat child sex trafficking and exploitation, creating a Tourism Child-Protection Code of Conduct endorsed by prominent hotel companies such as Hilton and Marriot and airlines such as Delta and American Airlines that addresses policy reform, training, education, and reporting.[154] However, the commitments under this code are voluntary, which limits their power and shields companies that turn a blind eye to commercial sex tourism with minors.[155] To better address these gaps, law enforcement agencies should improve collaboration to more effectively prosecute traffickers who perpetrate sexual exploitation of children in travel and tourism, and governments and the private sector should invest in research to identify effective prevention methods.

India

The ILO defines modern slavery as not only forced labor and debt bondage, but also as forced marriage—meaning a marriage entered into without consent, or when a party is under the age of eighteen, which is the internationally established minimum.[156] Roughly 15.4 million people are in forced marriages worldwide, with approximately one in three child brides residing in India, where 27 percent of girls are married before their eighteenth birthdays.[157] More than half of India's child brides live in just five states: Bihar, Madhya Pradesh, Maharashtra, Uttar Pradesh, and West Bengal.[158]

The forced marriage of Indian girls stems from poverty and the low status of girls and women, who receive less education and are viewed as a source of household labor, from housework to child and elder care.[159] The practice of *watta satta* is common in rural areas, wherein two families exchange girls through marriage so neither family is at a disadvantage in terms of household labor. Customary laws and social norms also contribute to early and forced marriage, with girls often married off in fear of a corrupted external environment, including rape in public spaces, which is viewed as an attack on a family's honor.[160] The belief that forced marriage protects young girls is belied by persistent evidence that child brides in India are at a greater risk of physical, sexual, and gender-based violence within their marital home than those not married as children.[161]

The sex ratio imbalance in India, which is fueled by female infanticide and sex-selective abortion practices that favor males, has also increased human trafficking for marriage.[162] The state of Haryana has only 830 girls for every thousand boys, leading men in northern India to purchase brides from other states. A 2014 Queens University survey of villages in Haryana and Rajasthan showed that the number of women in forced marriages increased by 30 percent over a three-year period, and the UN Office on Drugs and Crime (UNODC) pointed to criminal bride trafficking networks in the regions of Haryana, Punjab, and Uttar Pradesh, all of which have skewed gender ratios. Bride trafficking has proven to be so lucrative that locals set themselves up as brokers or dealers, arranging for women to be sold to families who are seeking wives for their sons.[163] UNODC reports that thousands of these women sold into marriages face abuse, rape, domestic slavery, and abandonment by their partners, who leave them to fend for themselves and their children.[164]

India has committed to eliminating child, early, and forced marriage by 2030, in line with a global commitment to eradicate forced marriage established in the global SDG framework, and has pledged to stem the tide of human trafficking.[165] However, to succeed, government efforts need to pursue not only law enforcement approaches that prosecute those in violation of underage marriage and human trafficking laws, but also cultural norms and customary practices that bolster forced marriage in the first place—particularly in places where these practices are most prevalent.

APPENDIX 2

PRIMARY GLOBAL AGREEMENTS
ON HUMAN TRAFFICKING AND FORCED LABOR

1930 **ILO Convention No. 29: Forced Labour Convention**
One of eight fundamental ILO conventions, the Forced Labour Convention defines forced labor as work performed involuntarily and under coercion. The convention requires states to suppress all forms of forced labor and enforce penalties.

1948 **UN Declaration of Human Rights (Article 4)**
Article 4 declares, "No one shall be held in slavery or servitude; slavery and the slave trade shall be prohibited in all their forms."

1949 **UN Convention for the Suppression of the Traffic in Persons and of the Exploitation of the Prostitution of Others**
This convention combats trafficking for prostitution and prohibits brothels. The preamble declares that trafficking for the purpose of prostitution is incompatible with human dignity and worth.

1966 **UN International Covenant on Civil and Political Rights (ICCPR)**
The ICCPR prohibits slavery, the slave trade, servitude, and forced labor, and guarantees many other civil and political rights.

1979 **UN Convention on the Elimination of All Forms of Discrimination against Women (CEDAW)**
A landmark bill of rights for women, CEDAW requires states to address the trafficking of women.

1998   ILO Declaration on Fundamental Principles and Rights at Work

This declaration requires ILO member states, even those that have not ratified relevant conventions, to take steps to protect freedom of association and the right of collective bargaining, and to eliminate forced labor, child labor, and discrimination in employment.

1999   ILO Convention 182: Elimination of Worst Forms of Child Labour

Convention 182 prohibits trafficking in children or forced labor, including recruitment of child soldiers, and obligates states to address child victims' well-being.

2000   Protocol to Prevent, Suppress and Punish Trafficking in Persons Especially Women and Children (Palermo Protocol)

The Palermo Protocol was a watershed moment in the fight against human trafficking and a supplement to the UN Convention against Transnational Organized Crime. Article 3 defines human trafficking as the transportation of persons by coercion for the purpose of exploitation. Article 5 requires states to criminalize trafficking. The accompanying Optional Protocol on the Sale of Children, Child Prostitution, and Child Pornography specifies forms of protection and assistance that states should make available to child victims.

2011   UN Guiding Principles on Business and Human Rights

The Guiding Principles are an implementation instrument of the United Nations' "Protect, Respect and Remedy" framework, which laid out a vision for how transnational corporations and other businesses should act with regard to human rights.

2014   ILO Protocol No. 29: Protocol of 2014 to the Forced Labour Convention, 1930

The International Labour Conference adopted a supplement to the 1930 convention by requiring states to take specific actions to eliminate human trafficking. Measures include providing victims with protection and access to remedies, sanctioning perpetrators, improving international coordination, and developing national prevention policies.

2000   **The Trafficking Victims Protection Act 2000 (TVPA)** was signed by President Bill Clinton on October 28, 2000, and had bipartisan support from Congress. It sought to strengthen the federal government's commitment to the Palermo Protocol by filling gaps in U.S. laws on trafficking, articulating a strategy with three main components: protection, prosecution, and prevention. It also codified new crimes relating to human trafficking, forced labor, and involuntary servitude; created new foreign and domestic anti-trafficking assistance programs; and established nonimmigrant status for victims that cooperated in investigating and prosecuting traffickers (T visas).

2003   **The 2003 TVPA reauthorization** created a new civil action enabling trafficking victims to sue their traffickers in federal district court, required annual progress reports from the U.S. attorney general, and called for greater dissemination of materials to alert travelers to the illegality of sex tourism.

2005   **The 2005 TVPA reauthorization** added protections for U.S. citizen survivors of human trafficking. It expanded victim assistance programs to U.S. citizens, increased comprehensive service and rehabilitation facilities for survivors, and established extraterritorial jurisdiction for trafficking offenses persons employed by or accompanying the federal government commit overseas.

2008   **The 2008 TVPA reauthorization,** also referred to as the William Wilberforce Trafficking Victims Protection Reauthorization Act, overhauled the Department of Justice legal requirements and penalties related to the facilitation of human trafficking, expanded victims' services provided by the Department of Health and Human Services, and elevated efforts by the Department of Labor to document and deter trafficking.

2013   **The 2013 TVPA reauthorization** strengthened programs to prevent U.S. citizens from purchasing products made by victims of human trafficking. It established Department of State emergency response provisions to facilitate rapid assistance to disaster areas and crises that fuel susceptibility to trafficking and strengthened prevention efforts against child soldiers and other forms of child trafficking. It also improved collaboration between state and local law enforcement to improve trafficking prosecutions.

2019   **The 2019 TVPA reauthorization** included H.R. 2200, the Frederick Douglass Trafficking Victims Prevention and Protection Reauthorization Act; S. 1311, the Abolish Human Trafficking Act; S. 1312, the Trafficking Victims Protection Act; and S. 1862, the Trafficking Victims Protection Reauthorization Act. These bills require the Justice Department to assign a human trafficking justice coordinator in each U.S. federal judicial district, instruct the Labor Department to include goods produced with materials that are made either wholly or in part by child or forced labor in its annual public reports, ban U.S. contractors from charging any recruitment fees to recruited employees, and require enhanced victim protection training for law enforcement officers.

ENDNOTES

1. International Labor Organization (ILO) and Walk Free Foundation, *Global Estimates of Modern Slavery: Forced Labour and Forced Marriage* (Geneva, 2017), 9, http://ilo.org/global/publications/books/WCMS_575479/lang--en/index.htm; and U.S. Department of State, *2020 Trafficking in Persons Report* (Washington, DC, 2020), http://state.gov/wp-content/uploads/2020/06/2020-TIP-Report-Complete-062420-FINAL.pdf.

2. ILO, *Profits and Poverty: The Economics of Forced Labour* (Geneva, 2014), 13, http://ilo.org/global/topics/forced-labour/publications/profits-of-forced-labour-2014/lang--en/index.htm. According to the ILO, approximately two-thirds of the estimated $150 billion in profits generated annually from human trafficking derives from sexual exploitation, with one-third stemming from economic exploitation, including domestic and agricultural labor. Although this figure is commonly cited, other related estimates exist and these figures would be strengthened by better monitoring and data collection, as recommended in this report.

3. UN Office on Drugs and Crime (UNODC), "Human Trafficking," accessed December 17, 2020, http://unodc.org/unodc/en/human-trafficking/what-is-human-trafficking.html.

4. UNODC, *An Introduction to Human Trafficking: Vulnerability, Impact and Action* (New York, 2008), 73, http://unodc.org/documents/human-trafficking/An_Introduction_to_Human_Trafficking_-_Background_Paper.pdf.

5. UNODC, *Global Report on Trafficking in Persons 2020* (Vienna, 2021), 95, http://unodc.org/documents/data-and-analysis/tip/2021/GLOTiP_2020_15jan_web.pdf.

6. UNODC, *Global Report on Trafficking in Persons 2020*, 59.

7. UNODC, *Global Report on Trafficking in Persons 2020*, 36; see also UNODC, "Human Trafficking FAQs," accessed February 12, 2021, http://unodc.org/unodc/en/human-trafficking/faqs.html.

8. John Cotton Richmond, "2020 TIP Report Celebrates 20 Years in the Fight to End Human Trafficking," U.S. Department of State, July 30, 2020, http://2017-2021.state.gov/2020-tip-report-celebrates-20-years-in-the-fight-to-end-human-trafficking//index.html.

9. Department of State, *2020 Trafficking in Persons Report*, Global Law Enforcement Data chart, 43.

10. ILO, "What Is Forced Labour, Modern Slavery and Human Trafficking?," http://ilo.org /global/topics/forced-labour/definition/lang--en/index.htm.

11. ILO, cited in Bureau of International Labor Affairs, "Child Labor, Forced Labor & Human Trafficking," accessed January 25, 2020, http://dol.gov/agencies/ilab/our-work /child-forced-labor-trafficking.

12. ILO, "More Than 60 Per Cent of the World's Employed Population Are in the Informal Economy," April 30, 2018, http://ilo.org/global/about-the-ilo/newsroom /news/WCMS_627189/lang--en/index.htm; and Organization for Economic Cooperation and Development (OECD) and ILO, "Tackling Vulnerability in the Informal Economy," http://oecd.org/fr/publications/tackling-vulnerability-in-the -informal-economy-939b7bcd-en.htm.

13. ILO and Walk Free Foundation, *Global Estimate,* 51.

14. Office of the United Nations High Commissioner for Human Rights (OHCHR), "Debt Bondage Remains the Most Prevalent Form of Forced Labour Worldwide – New UN Report," September 15, 2016, http://ohchr.org/EN/NewsEvents/Pages /DisplayNews.aspx?NewsID=20504&LangID.

15. UNODC, *The Role of Recruitment Fees and Abusive and Fraudulent Recruitment Practices of Recruitment Agencies in Trafficking in Persons* (Vienna, 2015), http://unodc .org/documents/human-trafficking/2015/Recruitment_Fees_Report-Final-22_June _2015_AG_Final.pdf.

16. For example, see Amnesty International, *'Their House Is My Prison': Exploitation of Migrant Domestic Workers in Lebanon* (London, 2019), http://amnesty.org/download /Documents/MDE1800222019ENGLISH.pdf.

17. UNODC, *Countering Trafficking in Persons in Conflict Situations* (Vienna, 2018), 15, http://unodc.org/documents/human-trafficking/2018/17-08776_ebook-Countering _Trafficking_in_Persons_in_Conflict_Situations.pdf.

18. UNODC, *Countering Trafficking in Persons in Conflict Situations*, 13.

19. ILO, "Child Labour and Armed Conflict," accessed December 17, 2020, http://ilo.org /ipec/areas/Armedconflict/lang--en/index.htm.

20. UNICEF, "Children Under Attack: Six Grave Violations Against Children in Times of War," September 27, 2018, http://unicef.org/stories/children-under-attack-six-grave -violations-against-children-times-war.

21. Cristina Rapone, "Migrant Workers and the COVID-19 Pandemic," Food and Agriculture Organization of the United Nations, April 7, 2020, http://fao.org/3 /ca8559en/CA8559EN.pdf; and ILO, "A Policy Framework for Tackling the Economic and Social Impact of the COVID-19 Crisis," May 2020, http://ilo.org/wcmsp5/groups /public/@dgreports/@dcomm/documents/briefingnote/wcms_745337.pdf.

22. Office of the UN High Commissioner for Human Rights (OHCHR), "Debt Bondage Remains the Most Prevalent Form of Forced Labor Worldwide," September 15, 2016, http://ohchr.org/en/NewsEvents/Pages/DisplayNews.aspx?NewsID=20504&LangID=E.

23. U.S. Department of Justice, "Human Trafficking," accessed December 17, 2020, http://justice.gov/humantrafficking.

24. ILO and Walk Free Foundation, *Global Estimates*, 5.

25. Polaris Project, "The Typology of Modern Slavery: Defining Sex and Labor Trafficking in the United States" (Washington, DC, 2017), 21, http://polarisproject.org/wp-content /uploads/2019/09/Polaris-Typology-of-Modern-Slavery-1.pdf.

26. Polaris Project, "The Typology of Modern Slavery"; and Polaris Project, "On-Ramps, Intersections, and Exit Routes: A Roadmap for Systems and Industries to Prevent and Disrupt Human Trafficking" (Washington, DC, 2018), http://polarisproject.org/wp -content/uploads/2018/08/A-Roadmap-for-Systems-and-Industries-to-Prevent-and -Disrupt-Human-Trafficking-Social-Media.pdf.International Justice Mission, *Online Sexual Exploitation of Children in the Philippines: Analysis and Recommendations for Governments, Industry, and Civil Society* (2020), 45, http://ijm.org/documents/studies /Final-Public-Full-Report-5_20_2020.pdf.

27. International Justice Mission, *Online Sexual Exploitation of Children in the Philippines: Analysis and Recommendations for Governments, Industry, and Civil Society* (2020), 45, http://ijm.org/documents/studies/Final-Public-Full-Report-5_20_2020.pdf.; Kieran Guilbert, "Women Sex Trafficked in UK Pop-up Brothels on an 'Industrial Scale,'" Reuters, May 21, 2018, http://reuters.com/article/us-britain-trafficking-sexcrimes /women-sex-trafficked-in-uk-pop-up-brothels-on-an-industrial-scale-idUSKCN1IM192.

28. Valiant Richey, "Statement by OSCE Special Representative for Combating Trafficking in Human Beings on Need to Strengthen Anti-trafficking Efforts in a Time of Crisis," Organization for Security and Cooperation in Europe, April 3, http://osce. org/secretariat/449554; and Louise Donovan and Corinne Redfern, "Coronavirus: Over 200% Surge in Links to Child Abuse Material Posted Online," Fuller Project, April 27, 2020, http://fullerproject.org/story/coronavirus-surge-child-abuse-material.

29. U.S. Department of Justice, "Thirty-Six Defendants Guilty for Their Roles in International Thai Sex Trafficking Organization," December 13, 2018, http://justice.gov/usao-mn/pr /thirty-six-defendants-guilty-their-roles-international-thai-sex-trafficking-organization.

30. United Nations High Commissioner for Refugees (UNHCR), "Child, Early and Forced Marriage, Including in Humanitarian Settings," accessed December 17, 2020, http://ohchr.org/EN/Issues/Women/WRGS/Pages/ChildMarriage.aspx.

31. ILO and Walk Free Foundation, *Global Estimates*, 11.

32. Several international agreements establish the definition of child marriage as a union in which one or both parties are under age eighteen and reinforce that consent is an essential component of marriage. The Convention on the Rights of the Child (1989) defines children as people who are under the age of eighteen. The Universal Declaration of Human Rights (1948) states that "men and women of full age" have the right to marry and affirms that "[m]arriage shall be entered into only with the free and full consent of the intending spouses." The Convention on Consent to Marriage, Minimum Age for Marriage, and Registration of Marriages (1962) calls on states to establish a minimum age of marriage and a system of registration. In addition, the Convention on the Elimination of All Forms of Discrimination Against Women (1979) proclaims that "the betrothal and marriage of a child shall have no legal effect"

and that women have a right to choose a spouse and enter into marriage with "free and full consent."

33. UNHCR, "Child, Early and Forced Marriage."

34. International Center for Research on Women, "Child Marriage Around the World," accessed December 17, 2020, http://icrw.org/child-marriage-facts-and-figures.

35. ILO and Walk Free Foundation, *Global Estimates.*

36. UNODC, *Interlinkages Between Trafficking in Persons and Marriage* (Vienna, 2020), http:// unodc.org/documents/human-trafficking/2020/UNODC_Interlinkages _Trafficking_in_Persons_and_Marriage.pdf.

37. UNICEF, "Child Marriage," April 2020, http://data.unicef.org/topic/child-protection /child-marriage.

38. Omer Karasapan and Sajjad Shah, "Forced Displacement and Child Marriage: A Growing Challenge in MENA," June 19, 2019, http://brookings.edu/blog/future-development /2019/06/19/forced-displacement-and-child-marriage-a-growing-challenge-in-mena.

39. United Nations Population Fund, "Impact of the COVID-19 Pandemic on Family Planning and Ending Gender-based Violence, Female Genital Mutilation and Child Marriage," Interim Technical Note, April 27, 2020, 2, http://unfpa.org/resources /impact-covid-19-pandemic-family-planning-and-ending-gender-based-violence -female-genital.

40. Jean Friedman-Rudovsky, "The Women Who Bear the Scars of Sierra Leone's Civil War," *Telegraph*, November 16, 2013, http://telegraph.co.uk/news/worldnews /africaandindianocean/sierraleone/10450619/The-women-who-bear-the-scars-of -Sierra-Leones-civil-war.html; and Gregory Warner, "Nigerian Abductions Part of a Terrible Pattern in African Conflicts," NPR, May 17, 2014, http://npr.org/sections /parallels/2014/05/17/313144946/nigerian-abductions-part-of-a-terrible-pattern-in -african-conflicts.

41. State Department, 2020 *Trafficking in Persons Report: Syria* (Washington, DC, 2020), http:// state.gov/reports/2020-trafficking-in-persons-report/syria; United Nations Assistance Mission for Iraq/UNHCR, *Report on the Protection of Civilians in Armed Conflict in Iraq,* (6 July–10 September 2014), 15, http://ohchr.org/Documents/Countries /IQ/UNAMI_OHCHR_POC_Report_FINAL_6July_10September2014.pdf; Human Rights Watch, "Iraq: ISIS Escapees Describe Systematic Rape," April 14, 2015, http:// hrw.org/news/2015/04/14/iraq-isis-escapees-describe-systematic-rape#; and State Department, "The Global Coalition to Counter ISIL," accessed December 23, 2020, http://2009-2017.state.gov/s/seci//index.htm.

42. UNODC, "Organ Trafficking," accessed February 10, 2019, http://unodc.org/unodc /en/organized-crime/intro/emerging-crimes/organ-trafficking.html.

43. UNODC, *Assessment Toolkit: Trafficking in Persons for the Purpose of Organ Removal* (Vienna, 2015), 28–29, http://unodc.org/documents/human-trafficking/2015 /UNODC_Assessment_Toolkit_TIP_for_the_Purpose_of_Organ_Removal.pdf.

44. Hannah Roberts, "Migrants Are Being Forced to Sell Their Organs to Pay for Being Trafficked From Africa to Europe," *Daily Mail*, October 13, 2014, http://dailymail.co.uk /news/article-2790949/migrants-forced-sell-organs-pay-trafficked-africa-europe.html.

Endnotes

45. Warren Strobel, Jonathan Landay, and Phil Stewart, "Exclusive: Islamic State Sanctioned Organ Harvesting in Document Taken in U.S. Raid," Reuters, December 24, 2015, http://reuters.com/article/us-usa-islamic-state-documents-idUSKBN0U805R20151225; U.S. Joint Counterterrorism Assessment Team, "First Responders' Toolbox: International Partnerships Among Public Health, Private Sector, and Law Enforcement Necessary to Mitigate ISIS's Organ Harvesting for Terrorist Funding," May 11, 2017, http://dni.gov/index.php/nctc-how-we-work/joint-ct-assessment-team/first-responder-toolbox; Ray Sanchez, "United Nations Investigates Claim of ISIS Organ Theft," CNN, February 19, 2015, http://cnn.com/2015/02/18/middleeast/isis-organ-harvesting-claim; and Anne Speckhard, "ISIS Defector Reports on the Sale of Organs Harvested From ISIS Held 'Slaves,'" *Huffington Post*, January 1, 2016, http://huffpost.com/entry/isis-defector-reports-on-sale-of-organs_b_8897708.

46. Channing May, *Transnational Crime and the Developing World* (Global Financial Integrity, 2017), 104, http://secureservercdn.net/45.40.149.159/34n.8bd.myftpupload.com/wp-content/uploads/2017/03/Transnational_Crime-final.pdf; Louise Shelley, *Dark Commerce: How a New Illicit Economy Is Threatening Our Future* (Princeton, NJ: Princeton University Press, 2018), chapter 6; and Channing Mavrellis, *Transnational Crime and the Developing World* (Washington, DC: Global Financial Integrity, March 2017), 29, http://gfintegrity.org/report/transnational-crime-and-the-developing-world.

47. Louise Shelley, *Dark Commerce*.

48. Sarah Bessell and Luz Nagle, *Human Trafficking and Public Corruption: A Report by the IBA's Presidential Task Force Against Human Trafficking* (London: International Bar Association, 2016), Human-trafficking-and-public-corruption-2016-FULL (1).pdf.

49. ILO, *Profits and Poverty*, 13.

50. Mavrellis, *Transnational Crime*.

51. June S. Beittel, "Mexico: Organized Crime and Drug Trafficking Organizations," CRS Report No. R41576 (Washington, DC, July 3, 2018), http://fas.org/sgp/crs/row/R41576.pdf.

52. Cynthia J. Arnson and Eric L. Olson, eds., *Organized Crime in Central America: The Northern Triangle* (Washington, DC: Latin American Program, Woodrow Wilson International Center for Scholars, September 2011), 184, http://wilsoncenter.org/publication/organized-crime-central-america-the-northern-triangle-no-29.

53. Giacomo Persi Paoli, Jacopo Bellasio, *Against the Rising Tide: An Overview of the Growing Criminalization of the Mediterranean Basin* (Santa Monica, CA: RAND Corporation, 2017), http://rand.org/content/dam/rand/pubs/perspectives/PE200/PE220/RAND_PE220.pdf; and Arnson and Olson, *Organized Crime in Central America*.

54. UNODC, "Global Report on Trafficking in Persons in the Context of Armed Conflict 2018" (Vienna, 2018), http://unodc.org/documents/data-and-analysis/glotip/2018/GloTIP2018_BOOKLET_2_Conflict_embargoed.pdf.

55. *Exploring the Financial Nexus of Terrorism, Drug Trafficking, and Organized Crime, Hearing Before the Terrorism and Illicit Finance Subcommittee, House Financial Services Committee*, 115th Cong. (2018) (statement of Louise Shelley, Professor and Chair at George Mason University's Schar School of Policy and International Affairs), http://financialservices.house.gov/uploadedfiles/03.20.2018_louise_shelley_testimony.pdf; and James Cockayne and Summer Walker, "Fighting Human Trafficking in Conflict,"

Workshop Report (United Nations University, 2016), http://unu.edu/fighting-human
-trafficking-in-conflict.

56. Michelle Nichols, "Russia, China Sent Home More Than Half of North Korean
Workers in 2018: U.N. Reports," Reuters, March 26, 2019, http://reuters.com
/article/us-northkorea-sanctions-un-exclusive/russia-china-sent-home-more-than
-half-of-north-korean-workers-in-2018-u-n-reports-idUSKCN1R70AT; Matthew
Zweig, "North Korea's Use of Slave Labor Will Limit Any Prospective Sanctions
Relief," Foundation for Defense of Democracies, February 27, 2019, http://fdd.org
/analysis/2019/02/27/north-koreas-use-of-slave-labor-will-limit-any-prospective
-sanctions-relief; Sarah Mendelson, "Outsourcing Oppression: Trafficked Labor from
North Korea," Foreign Affairs, May 28, 2015, http://foreignaffairs.com/articles/north
-korea/2015-05-28/outsourcing-oppression; State Department, *2018 Trafficking in
Persons Report: Democratic People's Republic of Korea* (Washington, DC, 2018), http://
state.gov/reports/2018-trafficking-in-persons-report/democratic-peoples-republic-of
-korea; and UN Security Council, Resolution 2397 (2017), S/RES/2397, http://unscr.
com/en/resolutions/doc/2397; and U.S. Mission to the United Nations, "Fact Sheet:
UN Security Council Resolution 2397 on North Korea," December 22, 2017, http://
usun.usmission.gov/fact-sheet-un-security-council-resolution-2397-on-north-korea.

57. ILO, "What Is Forced Labour, Modern Slavery and Human Trafficking"; and Vicky
Xiuzhong Xu et al., "Uyghurs for Sale: 'Re-education', Forced Labour and Surveillance
Beyond Xinjiang," Australian Strategic Policy Institute, March 1, 2020, http://aspi.org
.au/report/uyghurs-sale.

58. ILO and Walk Free Foundation, *Global Estimates*, 11.

59. António Guterres, "Conflict-Related Sexual Violence: Report of the United
Nations Secretary General" (New York: United Nations, 2020), http://un.org
/sexualviolenceinconflict/wp-content/uploads/2020/07/report/conflict-related-sexual
-violence-report-of-the-united-nations-secretary-general/2019-SG-Report.pdf.

60. Charles Anthony Smith and Heather M. Smith, "Human Trafficking: The Unintended
Effects of United Nations Intervention," *International Political Science Review* 32, no. 2
(2011): 125–45, http://journals.sagepub.com/doi/abs/10.1177/0192512110371240;
Sarah E. Mendelson, *Barracks and Brothels: Peacekeepers and Human Trafficking in the
Balkans* (Washington, DC: Center for Strategic and International Studies, February
2005), http://csis-prod.s3.amazonaws.com/s3fs-public/legacy_files/files/media/csis
/pubs/0502_barracksbrothels.pdf; and Sam R. Bell et al., "U.N. Peacekeeping Forces
and the Demand for Sex Trafficking," *International Studies Quarterly* 62, no. 3 (2018):
643–55, http://academic.oup.com/isq/article-abstract/62/3/643/5076386.

61. Donna M. Hughes, Katherine Y. Chon, and Derek P. Ellerman, "Modern-Day
Comfort Women: The U.S. Military, Transnational Crime, and the Trafficking of
Women," *Violence Against Women* 13, no. 9 (2007), http://journals.sagepub.com
/doi/10.1177/1077801207305218; David Vine, "My Body Was Not Mine, but the
US Military's: Inside the Disturbing Sex Industry Thriving Around America's Bases,"
Politico, November 3, 2015, http://politico.eu/article/my-body-was-not-mine-but
-the-u-s-militarys.; Samantha T. Godec, "Between Rhetoric and Reality: Exploring the
Impact of Military Humanitarian Intervention Upon Sexual Violence – Post-Conflict
Sex Trafficking in Kosovo," (International Committee of the Red Cross, March 2010),
http://icrc.org/en /international-review/article/between-rhetoric-and

-reality-exploring-impact-military-humanitarian; Stop Violence Against Women, "Protecting the Human Rights of Women and Girls Trafficked for Forced Prostitution in Kosovo" (Amnesty International, May 2004), http://amnesty.org/download /Documents/96000/eur700102004en.pdf; Charles Anthony Smith and Miller de la Cuesta, "Human Trafficking in Conflict Zones," *Human Rights Review* 12 (2011): 287–99; and Olivier Peyroux, "Trafficking in Human Beings in Conflict and Post-Conflict Situation," *Caritas*, June 2015, http://caritas.org /wordpress/wp-content /uploads/2015/06/RESEARCH-ACTION-Trafficking-in-human-beings-and -conflicts-EN-10-juin-2015.pdf.

62. Human Rights Watch, "Hopes Betrayed: Trafficking of Women and Girls to Post-Conflict Bosnia and Herzegovina for Forced Prostitution," *Bosnia and Herzegovina* 14, no. 9(D) (November 2002), http://hrw.org/reports/2002/bosnia/Bosnia1102.pdf.

63. ILO, *The Cost of Coercion* (Geneva, 2009), 32, http://ilo.org/wcmsp5/groups/public /---ed_norm/---declaration/documents/publication/wcms_106268.pdf. This is the most recent estimate.

64. Liechtenstein Initiative, *A Blueprint for Mobilizing Finance Against Slavery and Trafficking* (New York: United Nations University Centre for Policy Research, 2019), 22, http://fastinitiative.org/wp-content/uploads/Blueprint-DIGITAL-3.pdf.

65. Pritha Mitra, Eric N. Pondi Endengle, Malika Pant, and Luiz F. Almeida, "Does Child Marriage Matter for Growth?" IMF Working Paper No. 20/27, February 7, 2020, 5, http://imf.org/en/Publications/WP/Issues/2020/02/08/Does-Child-Marriage-Matter -for-Growth-49011.

66. ILO, *Ending Forced Labour by 2030: A Review of Policies and Programmes* (Geneva, 2018), http://ilo.org/wcmsp5/groups/public/---ed_norm/---ipec/documents /publication/wcms_653986.pdf.

67. Liechtenstein Initiative, *Blueprint for Mobilizing Finance.*

68. Erica G. Polakoff, "Globalization and Child Labor: Review of the Issues," *Journal of Developing Societies* 23, no. 1-2 (2007): 259–83, http://journals.sagepub.com/doi/10 .1177/0169796X0602300215.

69. Devin Brewer, "Globalization and Human Trafficking," *Topical Research Digest: Human Rights and Human Trafficking*, 46–58, http://du.edu/korbel/hrhw/researchdigest /trafficking/Globalization.pdf.

70. ILO, "Ratifications of C029 - Forced Labour Convention, 1930 (No. 29)," accessed January 19, 2020, http://ilo.org/dyn/normlex/en/f?p=1000:11300:0::NO:11300 :P11300_INSTRUMENT_ID:312174; and Dursun Peksen and Robert G. Blanton, "The Impact of ILO conventions on Worker Rights: Are Empty Promises Worse Than No Promises?" *Review of International Organizations* 12 (2017): 75–94, http://link .springer.com/article/10.1007%2Fs11558-015-9241-9.

71. See, for example, James Cockayne, *Developing Freedom: The Sustainable Development Case for Ending Modern Slavery, Forced Labour and Human Trafficking* (New York: United Nations University, 2021).

72. UNODC, "An Introduction to Human Trafficking: Vulnerability, Impact and Action," 2008, http://unodc.org/documents/human-trafficking/An_Introduction_to_Human_ Trafficking_-_Background_Paper.pdf; and Charlotte Lindsey Curtet, Florence Tercier

Holst-Roness, and Letitia Anderson, "Addressing the Needs of Women Affected by Armed Conflict: An ICRC Guidance Document" (International Committee of the Red Cross, March 2004), http://icrc.org/en/doc/assets/files/other/icrc_002_0840 _women_guidance.pdf.

73. OHCHR, "Debt Bondage Remains the Most Prevalent Form of Forced Labour Worldwide – New UN Report," September 15, 2016, http://ohchr.org/en/NewsEvents /Pages/DisplayNews.aspx?NewsID=20504&LangID=E.

74. UN Security Council, Resolution 2331 (2016), S/RES/2331.

75. UNODC, Transnational Organized Crime in Central America and the Caribbean: A Threat Assessment; UNHCR, "Guidance Note on Refugee Claims Relating to Victims of Organized Gangs," March 31, 2010, http://refworld.org/docid/4bb21fa02.html; and UNHCR, "Women on the Run: First-Hand Accounts of Refugees Fleeing El Salvador, Guatemala, Honduras, and Mexico," October 2015, http://unhcr.org/5630f24c6.pdf.

76. OECD, "Trafficking in Persons: Weak Governance and Growing Profits," in Trafficking in Persons and Corruption: Breaking the Chain (Paris: OECD Publishing, 2016), 11–31, http://oecd-ilibrary.org/docserver/9789264253728-en.pdf; and Katharina Hofmann, "The Impact of Organized Crime on Democratic Governance – Focus on Latin America and the Caribbean" (Fredrich Ebert Stiftung, September 2009), http://library.fes.de /pdf-files/iez/global/06697.pdf.

77. The ILO adopted its Forced Labour Convention in 1930 to eliminate forced or compulsory labor in all its forms and its Worst Forms of Child Labour Convention in 1999 to eliminate all forms of slavery and trafficking of children, as well as the commercial sexual exploitation of children.

78. Richard Boucher, "Press Statement: President's Interagency Task Force to Monitor and Combat Trafficking in Persons," State Department, February 14, 2002, http:// 2001-2009.state.gov/r/pa/prs/ps/2002/8031.htm; and White House, "Fact Sheet: Building a Lasting Effort to End Modern Slavery," October 24, 2016, http:// obamawhitehouse.archives.gov/the-press-office/2016/10/24/fact-sheet-building -lasting-effort-end-modern-slavery.

79. White House, "Executive Order 13627 of September 25, 2012, Strengthening Protections Against Trafficking in Persons in Federal Contracts," Code of Federal Regulations, title 3 (2012): 1–5, http://govinfo.gov/content/pkg/DCPD-201200750 /pdf/DCPD-201200750.pdf; and State Department, 2019 Report on U.S. Government Efforts to Combat Trafficking in Persons (Washington, DC, 2019), http://state.gov/2019 -report-on-u-s-government-efforts-to-combat-trafficking-in-persons.

80. White House, "The National Action Plan to Combat Human Trafficking" (Washington, DC, 2020), http://trumpwhitehouse.archives.gov/wp-content/uploads/2020/10/NAP -to-Combat-Human-Trafficking.pdf.

81. Judith Kelley, Scorecard Diplomacy: Grading State to Influence Their Reputation and Behavior (New York: Cambridge University Press, 2017).

82. Department of Labor, 2020 List of Goods Produced by Child Labor or Forced Labor (Washington, DC, September 2020), http://dol.gov/sites/dolgov/files/ILAB/child _labor_reports/tda2019/2020_TVPRA_List_Online_Final.pdf.

83. Financial Crimes Enforcement Network, "Supplemental Advisory on Identifying and Reporting Human Trafficking and Related Activity," U.S. Department of the Treasury, October 15, 2020, http://fincen.gov/sites/default/files/advisory/2020-10-15/Advisory%20Human%20Trafficking%20508%20FINAL_0.pdf; Financial Crimes Enforcement Network, "Guidance on Recognizing Activity That May be Associated With Human Smuggling and Human Trafficking –Financial Red Flags," U.S. Department of the Treasury, September 11, 2014, http://fincen.gov/resources/advisories/fincen-advisory-fin-2014-a008.

84. Liechtenstein Initiative, *Blueprint for Mobilizing Finance*.

85. Office of Senator Mark Warner, "Warner, Rounds, Jones Applaud Inclusion of Bipartisan Anti-Money Laundering Legislation in NDAA," December 3, 2020, http://warner.senate.gov/public/index.cfm/pressreleases?ID=748756D0-DE6C-4B31-960E-AAFD205AAF6B.

86. ILO, "ILO Standards on Forced Labour: The New Protocol and Recommendation at a Glance" (Geneva, November 8, 2016), http://ilo.org/global/topics/forced-labour/publications/WCMS_508317/lang--en/index.htm.

87. Government of Australia, Modern Slavery Act, 2018, no. 153, http://legislation.gov.au/Details/C2018A00153; Government of the United Kingdom, Modern Slavery Act of 2015 (UK Public General Acts), http://legislation.gov.uk/ukpga/2015/30/contents/enacted; and California Transparency in Supply Chains Act (California, S.B. 657), http://oag.ca.gov/SB657.

88. Government of France, LOI n° 2017-399 du 27 mars 2017 relative au devoir de vigilance des sociétés mères et des entreprises donneuses d'ordre (1), http://legifrance.gouv.fr/jorf/id/JORFTEXT000034290626; Government of the Netherlands, Wet van 24 oktober 2019 houdende de invoering van een zorgplicht ter voorkoming van de levering van goederen en diensten die met behulp van kinderarbeid tot stand zijn gekomen (Wet zorgplicht kinderarbeid), http://zoek.officielebekendmakingen.nl/stb-2019-401.html; Frank Specht, "Heil und Müller entschärfen die Haftungsregeln für Unternehmen," Handelsblatt, June 25, 2020, http://handelsblatt.com/politik/deutschland/lieferkettengesetz-heil-und-mueller-entschaerfen-die-haftungsregeln-fuer-unternehmen/25947310.html; and Sandra Cossart and Lucie Chatelain, "What Lessons Does France's Duty of Vigilance Law Have for Other National Initiatives?" Business and Human Rights Resource Center, June 27, 2019, http://business-humanrights.org/en/blog/what-lessons-does-frances-duty-of-vigilance-law-have-for-other-national-initiatives.

89. Policy Department for External Relations, *Human Rights Due Diligence Legislation: Options for the EU* (Brussels: European Union, 2020), http://europarl.europa.eu/RegData/etudes/BRIE/2020/603495/EXPO_BRI(2020)603495_EN.pdf; and Maria Grazia Giammarinaro, "Report of the Special Rapporteur on Trafficking in Persons, Especially Women and Children," A/HRC/44/45 (New York: United Nations, April 6, 2020), 13, http://undocs.org/en/A/HRC/44/45.

90. State Department, 2020 *Trafficking in Persons Report*, 45–46; and Gregory E. van der Vink, Katherine N. Carlson, Jeffrey Park, Sabrina H. Szeto, Xinrei Zhang, Michael E. Jackson , and Erica Phillips, "Empirical Analysis of the U.S. State Department's Annual Trafficking in Persons Report – Insights for Policy-Makers," *Journal of Human Trafficking* (2021):2, http://doi.org/10.1080/23322705.2021.1897759.

91. Department of State, *2020 Trafficking in Persons Report*, 40–41.

92. Sarah Mendelson, "Combating Human Trafficking and the Biden Administration," Council on Foreign Relations (blog), January 28, 2021, http://cfr.org/blog/combating -human-trafficking-and-biden-administration; James Cockayne, "What Role Should Anti-Trafficking Play in U.S. Development Efforts?" Council on Foreign Relations, February 8, 2021, http://cfr.org/blog/what-role-should-anti-trafficking-play-us -development-efforts; and Oliva Enos and Mark Lagon, "Revitalizing Human Trafficking Policy Twenty Years In," Council on Foreign Relations (blog), October 21, 2020, http://cfr.org/blog/revitalizing-human-trafficking-policy-twenty-years.

93. U.S. Department of Treasury, "Treasury Sanctions Individuals and Companies Associated with Japan's Major Organized Crime Syndicate, the Yakuza," October 2, 2018, http://home.treasury.gov/news/press-releases/sm499; Office of the White House, *The National Action Plan to Combat Human Trafficking* (Washington, DC: 2020), http://trumpwhitehouse.archives.gov/wp-content/uploads/2020/10/NAP-to -Combat-Human-Trafficking.pdf.

94. State Department, "Report to Congress on An Analysis of Anti-Money Laundering Efforts Related to Human Trafficking Section 7154(a) of the National Defense Authorization Act for Fiscal Year 2020," Div. F., P.L. 116-92 (Washington, DC, 2020), http://state.gov/wp-content/uploads/2020/10/Final-AML-Report-to-Congress.pdf.

95. International Organization for Migration, *World Migration Report* (Geneva, 2020), http://publications.iom.int/system/files/pdf/wmr_2020.pdf.

96. Courtney Bublé, "Federal Contract Spending Reaches Its Highest Level Ever in Fiscal 2019, Marking 4 Straight Years of Growth," *Government Executive*, June 26, 2020, http://govexec.com/management/2020/06/federal-contract-spending-reaches-its -highest-level-ever-fiscal-2019-marking-4-straight-years-growth/166484.

97. Department of Defense Inspector General, "Evaluation of DoD Efforts to Combat Trafficking in Persons in Kuwait DODIG-2019-088," June 11, 2019, http://dodig.mil /reports.html/Article/1874544/evaluation-of-dod-efforts-to-combat-trafficking-in -persons-in-kuwait-dodig-2019/; United States Department of Justice, *Assessment of U.S. Government Efforts to Combat Trafficking in Persons in Fiscal Year 2006* (Washington, DC: 2006), http://justice.gov/archive/ag/annualreports/tr2007 /assessment-of-efforts-to-combat-tip0907.pdf.

98. Alliance to End Slavery and Trafficking (ATEST), "ATEST Provides Preliminary Comments on USAID C-TIP Policy Revision," December 18, 2020, http:// endslaveryandtrafficking.org/atest-provides-preliminary-comments-on-usaid-c-tip -policy-revision.

99. Sarah Mendelson, "Combating Human Trafficking and the Biden Administration," Council on Foreign Relations (blog), January 28, 2021, http://cfr.org/blog/combating -human-trafficking-and-biden-administration.

100. State Department, *2020 Trafficking in Persons Report*, 43.

101. State Department, *2020 Trafficking in Persons Report*, 515–16.

102. Dave Shaw and Travis Frugé, *Child Sex Trafficking in Metro Manila* (Washington, DC: International Justice Mission, 2016), http://ijm.org/documents/studies/ijm-manila

-final-web-v2.pdf; Dave Shaw and Travis Frugé, *Child Sex Trafficking in Angeles City* (Washington, DC: International Justice Mission, 2016), http://ijm.org/documents /studies/ijm-pampanga-final-web-pdf-v2.pdf; International Justice Mission, "International Justice Mission Cebu, the Philippines Project Lantern Results Summary," January 2011, http://ijm.org/documents/studies/Cebu-Project-Lantern-Results -Summary.pdf; and Robin Haarr, *External Evaluation of International Justice Mission's Program to Combat Sex Trafficking of Children in Cambodia, 2004–2014* (Washington, DC: International Justice Mission, 2015), http://ijm.org/documents/studies/2015 -Evaluation-of-IJM-CSEC-Program-in-Cambodia-Final-Report.pdf.

103. Anasuya Syam and Meg Roggensack, "Importing Freedom: Using the U.S. Tariff Act to Combat Forced Labor in Supply Chains" (Human Trafficking Legal Center, 2020), 39, http://htlegalcenter.org/wp-content/uploads/Importing-Freedom-Using-the-U.S. -Tariff-Act-to-Combat-Forced-Labor-in-Supply-Chains_FINAL.pdf; and U.S. Government Accountability Office, "Better Communication Could Improve Trade Enforcement Efforts Related to Seafood," GAO-20-441 (Washington, DC, 2020), http://gao .gov/assets/710/707686.pdf.

104. *Nestlé USA, Inc. v. Doe I and Cargill Inc. v. Doe I*, brief amicus curiae of Trump administration, May 20, 2020, http://supremecourt.gov/DocketPDF/19/19-453/144200 /20200526124902074_Nestle.Cargill%20final.pdf.

105. James Cockayne, *Developing Freedom: The Sustainable Development Case for Ending Modern Slavery*, Forced Labour and Human Trafficking (New York: United Nations University, 2021).

106. James Cockayne, *Developing Freedom*, 32; James Cockayne, "ODA Spending on Modern Slavery: Donors," Developing Freedom, citing AidData Institute, University of William and Mary, accessed March 18, 2021, http://developingfreedom.org/oda -spending-donors.

107. Sophie Otiende and Ayesha Lissanevitch, "Why Data: The Importance of Systematizing Data Capture," Delta 8.7, October 14, 2020, http://delta87.org/2020/10/why-data -importance-systematizing-data-capture.

108. Institute for Human Rights and Business, "Dhaka Principles for Migration With Dignity," accessed December 23, 2020, http://ihrb.org/dhaka-principles.

109. Migration That Works, "Proposal for an Alternative Model for Labor Migration," accessed February 1, 2021, http://migrationthatworks.files.wordpress.com/2020/01 /alternative-model-for-labor-migration.pdf; and International Labor Recruitment Working Group, "The American Dream Up for Sale: A Blueprint for Ending International Labor Recruitment Abuse" (Washington, DC, 2013), http://aft.org/sites/default/files /wysiwyg/international_labor_recruitment_abuse.pdf.

110. Biden-Harris, "The Biden Plan for Securing Our Values as a Nation of Immigrants," accessed December 23, 2020, http://joebiden.com/immigration.

111. Giammarinaro, "Report of the Special Rapporteur."

112. Sarah Dadush, "Contracting for Human Rights: Looking to Version 2.0 of the ABA Model Contract Clauses," *American University Law Review* 68, no. 1519 (2019), http:// papers.ssrn.com/sol3/papers.cfm?abstract_id=3420479; and Frederick Douglass

Trafficking Victims Prevention and Protection Reauthorization Act of 2018, Pub. L. 115-425, 132 Statute 5472, January 8, 2019, http://congress.gov/115/plaws/publ425 /PLAW-115publ425.pdf.

113. Cockayne, *Developing Freedom*; and Sarah Mendelson, "Combating Human Trafficking and the Biden Administration," Council on Foreign Relations (blog), January 28, 2021, http://cfr.org/blog/combating-human-trafficking-and-biden-administration; and State Department, "Report to Congress on An Analysis of Anti-Money Laundering Efforts Related to Human Trafficking Section 7154(a) of the National Defense Authorization Act for Fiscal Year 2020," Div. F., Pub. L. 116-92 (Washington, DC, 2020), http://state .gov/wp-content/uploads/2020/10/Final-AML-Report-to-Congress.pdf.

114. *Stop Predatory Organ Trafficking Act of 2020,* HR 7805, 116th Cong., July 27, 2020, http://congress.gov/bill/116th-congress/house-bill/7805.

115. David Kennedy and Dan Danielsen, "Busting Bribery: Sustaining the Global Momentum of the Foreign Corrupt Practices Act," Open Society Foundations, September 2011, http://opensocietyfoundations.org/publications/busting-bribery -sustaining-global-momentum-foreign-corrupt-practices-act.

116. George Serafeim, "Social-Impact Efforts That Create Real Value," *Harvard Business Review*, September-October 2020, http://hbr.org/2020/09/social-impact-efforts-that -create-real-value; and State Department, "Anti-Money Laundering and Countering the Financing of Terrorism," accessed February 1, 2021, http://state.gov/anti-money -laundering-and-countering-the-financing-of-terrorism.

117. Anasuya Syam and Meg Roggensack, "Importing Freedom: Using the U.S. Tariff Act to Combat Forced Labor in Supply Chains" (Washington, DC: Human Trafficking Legal Center, 2020), http://htlegalcenter.org/wp-content/uploads/Importing-Freedom-Using -the-U.S.-Tariff-Act-to-Combat-Forced-Labor-in-Supply-Chains_FINAL.pdf.

118. GAO, "Forced Labor Imports: DHS Increased Resources and Enforcement Efforts, but Needs to Improve Workforce Planning and Monitoring," GAO-21-106 (Washington, DC, October 2020), http://gao.gov/assets/720/710343.pdf.

119. Office of Representative Earl Blumenauer (D-OR), "Chairman Blumenauer Files Legislation to Update Key Trade Program," December 8, 2020, http://blumenauer .house.gov/media-center/press-releases/chairman-blumenauer-files-legislation -update-key-trade-program; and Office of Senator Bob Casey (D-PA), "Casey, Cortez Masto Introduce Legislation to Push for Women's Rights in International Trade," June 18, 2020, http://casey.senate.gov/newsroom/releases/casey-cortez-masto-introduce -legislation-to-push-for-womens-rights-in-international-trade.

120. State Department, *2020 Trafficking in Persons Report,* 515; and Martina Vandenberg and Sarah Bessell, "Diplomatic Immunity and the Abuse of Domestic Workers: Criminal and Civil Remedies in the United States," *Duke Journal of Comparative & International Law* 26 (2016): 595–633, http://scholarship.law.duke.edu/djcil/vol26/iss3/6.

121. Giammarinaro, "Report of the Special Rapporteur"; and ILO, OECD, IOM, and UNICEF, *Ending Child Labour, Forced Labour and Human Trafficking in Global Supply Chains* (New York, 2019), 39.

122.	Alliance to End Slavery & Trafficking, "Fiscal Year 2022 Federal Appropriations Recommendations," accessed April 14, 2021, http://endslaveryandtrafficking.org /appropriations-guide; and Sarah Mendelson, "Combating Human Trafficking and the Biden Administration," Council on Foreign Relations (blog), January 28, 2021, http://cfr.org/blog/combating-human-trafficking-and-biden-administration; and State Department, "Report to Congress on An Analysis of Anti-Money Laundering Efforts Related to Human Trafficking Section 7154(a) of the National Defense Authorization Act for Fiscal Year 2020," Div. F., Pub. L. 116-92 (Washington, DC, 2020), http:// state.gov/wp-content/uploads/2020/10/Final-AML-Report-to-Congress.pdf.

123.	Dan Viederman, "How Innovation Can Help End Forced Labor in Global Supply Chains," *Women Around the World,* Council on Foreign Relations (blog), December 7, 2020, http:// cfr.org/blog/how-innovation-can-help-end-forced-labor-global-supply-chains.

124.	DNA tracing can identify the source of a product and its stops along the supply chain—using stable isotopes, in the case of Britain, or the DNA on the dust found on products, as Phylagen does—which offers the potential of enabling governments and multinationals to avoid costly and time-consuming chain-of-custody audits or the uncertainty of supplier assurances. Artificial intelligence and machine learning could allow governments and multinationals to predict forced labor risks across an entire supply chain, enabling them to prioritize ethical suppliers; a new decision support tool, for example—developed by the Global Fund to End Modern Slavery and to be released open source—has 84 percent accuracy in identifying forced labor risks. See Global Fund to End Modern Slavery, "GFEMS Wins Innovation Award for Forced Labor Risk Detection Tool," accessed December 23, 2020, http://gfems.org/news/2020/10/14 /gfems-wins-innovation-award-for-forced-labor-risk-detection-tool.

125.	Cockayne, *Developing Freedom.*

126.	State Department, *2020 Trafficking in Persons Report*, 156.

127.	State Department, *2020 Trafficking in Persons Report*, 156.

128.	Department of Labor, *2020 List of Goods Produced by Child Labor or Forced Labor* (Washington, DC, September 2020), 28, http://dol.gov/sites/dolgov/files/ILAB/child _labor_reports/tda2019/2020_TVPRA_List_Online_Final.pdf.

129.	Congressional-Executive Commission on China, "Prospects for Reforming China's Reeducation Through Labor System" (Washington, DC, 2013), http://cecc.gov /publications/issue-papers/prospects-for-reforming-chinas-reeducation-through -labor-system.

130.	Wu Jiao, "New Law to Abolish Laojiao System," March 1, 2007, http://chinadaily.com .cn/china/2007-03/01/content_816358.htm; and State Department, *2014 Trafficking in Persons Report: Country Narratives* (Washington, DC, June 2013), 132, http://2009 -2017.state.gov/documents/organization/226845.pdf.

131.	State Department, *2015 Trafficking in Persons Report* (Washington, DC, 2015), 120, http://2009-2017.state.gov/documents/organization/245365.pdf; and John Ruwitch, "A Jail by Another Name: China Labor Camps Now Drug Detox Centers," Reuters, December 2, 2013, http://reuters.com/article/us-china-camps/a-jail-by-another-name -china-labor-camps-now-drug-detox-centers-idUSBRE9B10CQ20131202.

132. Vicky Xiuzhong Xu et al., *Uyghurs for Sale: 'Re-education', Forced Labour and Surveillance Beyond Xinjiang,* Australian Strategic Policy Institute, March 1, 2020, http://aspi.org.au/report/uyghurs-sale.

133. Vicky Xiuzhong Xu et al., *Uyghurs for Sale*; Eva Dou and Chao Deng, "Western Companies Get Tangled in China's Muslim Clampdown," *Wall Street Journal,* May 16, 2019, http://wsj.com/articles/western-companies-get-tangled-in-chinas-muslim-clampdown-11558017472.

134. Amy Lehr, "Addressing Forced Labor in the Xinjiang Uyghur Autonomous Region: Toward a Shared Agenda," Center for Strategic & International Studies, July 30, 2020, http://csis.org/analysis/addressing-forced-labor-xinjiang-uyghur-autonomous-region-toward-shared-agenda; and Ana Swanson, "U.S. May Ban Cotton From Xinjiang Region of China Over Rights Concerns," *New York Times*, September 7, 2020, http://nytimes.com/2020/09/07/business/economy/us-china-xinjiang-cotton-ban.html.

135. U.S. Customs and Border Patrol, "CBP Issues Region-Wide Withhold Release Order on Products Made by Slave Labor in Xinjiang," January 13, 2021, http://cbp.gov/newsroom/national-media-release/cbp-issues-region-wide-withhold-release-order-products-made-slave.

136. U.S. Customs and Border Patrol, "CBP Issues Region-Wide Withhold Release Order"; International Labor Rights Forum, "Human Rights Groups Call on US for Regional Ban on Imports From China Made With Uyghur Forced Labor," August 31, 2020, http://laborrights.org/releases/human-rights-groups-call-us-regional-ban-imports-china-made-uyghur-forced-labor.

137. Uyghur Human Rights Policy Act of 2020, Pub. L. No. 116-145, 134 Stat. 648 (2020).

138. Jasper Gilardi, "Ally or Exploiter? The Smuggler-Migrant Relationship Is a Complex One," Migration Policy Institute, February 5, 2020, http://migrationpolicy.org/article/ally-or-exploiter-smuggler-migrant-relationship-complex-one; and UNODC, "UNODC on trafficking in persons and smuggling of migrants," accessed December 15, 2020, http://unodc.org/unodc/en/human-trafficking/index.html?ref=menuside.

139. United States Citizenship and Immigration Services (USCIS), "Victims of Human Trafficking: T Nonimmigrant Status," May 10, 2018, http://uscis.gov/humanitarian/victims-of-human-trafficking-and-other-crimes/victims-of-human-trafficking-t-nonimmigrant-status.

140. Jenna Krajeski, "The Hypocrisy of Trump's Anti-Trafficking Argument for a Border Wall," *New Yorker,* February 5, 2019, http://newyorker.com/news/news-desk/the-hypocrisy-of-trumps-anti-trafficking-argument-for-a-border-wall; State Department, *2020 Trafficking in Persons Report*; and Abigail Adams, "'I Thought I Was Going to Die.' How Donald Trump's Immigration Agenda Set Back the Clock on Fighting Human Trafficking," *Time*, October 30, 2020, http://time.com/5905437/human-trafficking-trump-administration.

141. USCIS, "Number of Form I-918, Petition for U Nonimmigrant Status," 2020, http://uscis.gov/sites/default/files/document/reports/I918u_visastatistics_fy2020_qtr3.pdf.

142. USCIS, "U Visa Filing Trends," April 2020, http://uscis.gov/sites/default/files/document/reports/Mini_U_Report-Filing_Trends_508.pdf; and U.S. Immigration and Customs Enforcement, "Revision of Stay of Removal Request Reviews for U

Visa Petitioners," Fact Sheet, August 2, 2019, http://ice.gov/factsheets/revision-stay
-removal-request-reviews-u-visa-petitioners.

143. Amnesty International, "Migration: To/From/In: A Middle East and North Africa
Story," accessed December 16, 2020, http://amnesty.org/en/latest/campaigns/2018/12
/migration-to-from-in-middle-east-north-africa.

144. Amnesty International, "Migration: To/From/In."

145. Amnesty International, *Their House Is My Prison.*

146. Amnesty International, *Their House Is My Prison.*

147. Human Rights Watch, "Qatar: Significant Labor and Kafala Reforms," September 24,
2020, http://hrw.org/news/2020/09/24/qatar-significant-labor-and-kafala-reforms.

148. BBC, "Saudi Arabia Eases 'Kafala' System Restrictions on Migrant Workers,"
November 4, 2020, http://bbc.com/news/world-middle-east-54813515; and
Vivian Nereim, "Saudi Arabia Loosens Controversial Curbs on Foreign Workers,"
Bloomberg, November 4, 2020, http://bloomberg.com/news/articles/2020-11-04
/saudi-arabia-eases-controversial-restrictions-on-foreign-workers.

149. State Department, *2020 Trafficking in Persons Report,* 119.

150. Natasha Dolby, "Domestic Sex Trafficking of Children in Brazil" (WSD Handa Center
for Human Rights and International Justice, Stanford University, 2018), 13–14, http://
humanrights.stanford.edu/sites/g/files/sbiybj5951/f/publications/domestic_child
_trafficking_brazil_dolby_final_report.pdf.

151. UNODC, "Brazilian Senate Approves Law With Harsher Punishments for the Crime
of Human Trafficking," September 16, 2016, http://unodc.org/lpo-brazil/en/frontpage
/2016/09/05-brazilian-senate-approves-law-with-harsher-punishments-for-the-crime
-of-human-trafficking.html; and Dolby, "Domestic Sex Trafficking," 5.

152. State Department, *2020 Trafficking in Persons Report,* 118; and Dolby, "Domestic Sex
Trafficking," 27.

153. ECPAT Brazil, *Country Specific Report: Brazil* (2015), 13; and Dolby, "Domestic Sex
Trafficking," 24.

154. ECPAT USA, "The Tourism Child-Protection Code of Conduct," accessed January 25,
2021, http://ecpatusa.org/code#:~:text=The%20Tourism%20Child%2DProtection
%20Code%20of%20Conduct%20(The%20Code),the%20travel%20and%20
hospitality%20industry.

155. Ann Brooks and Vanessa Heaslip, "Sex Trafficking and Sex Tourism in a Globalised
World," *Tourism Review* 74, no. 2 (2018), http://emerald.com/insight/content/doi/10
.1108/TR-02-2017-0017/full/html.

156. ILO and Walk Free Foundation, *Global Estimates of Modern Slavery.*

157. ILO and Walk Free Foundation, *Global Estimates,* 43; UNICEF, "Ending Child Marriage: A Profile of Progress in India," 2019, http://unicef.org/india/media/1176/file
/Ending-Child-Marriage.pdf; and Girls Not Brides, "India," accessed December 17,
2020, http://girlsnotbrides.org/child-marriage/india.

158. UNICEF, "Ending Child Marriage."

159. Girls Not Brides, "India."

160. Girls Not Brides, "India."

161. Rachel Kidman, "Child Marriage and Intimate Partner Violence: A Comparative Study of 34 Countries," *International Journal of Epidemiology* 46, no. 2 (2017): 662–75, http://academic.oup.com/ije/article/46/2/662/2417355.

162. Sreya Banerjea, "Harrowing True Stories of India's Trafficked Brides," *Independent*, October 3, 2020, http://independent.co.uk/news/long_reads/world/india-trafficked -brides-marriage-abuse-crime-domestic-b737919.html.

163. Anu Anand, "India's Bride Trafficking Fueled by Skewed Sex Ratios," *The Guardian,* December 17, 2014, http://theguardian.com/global-development/2014/dec/17/india -bride-trafficking-foeticide.

164. UNODC, "India Country Assessment Report: Current Status of Victim Service Providers and Criminal Justice Actors on Anti Human Trafficking," 2013, http:// unodc.org/documents/southasia/reports/Human_Trafficking-10-05-13.pdf.

165. National Institution for Transforming India, "SDG India: Index and Dashboard," 2019, http://niti.gov.in/sites/default/files/SDG-India-Index-2.0_27-Dec.pdf.

ABOUT THE AUTHORS

Jamille Bigio is a senior fellow for the Women and Foreign Policy program at the Council on Foreign Relations. Previously, she was director for human rights and gender on the White House National Security Council staff, served on the White House Council on Women and Girls, and advised the office of First Lady Michelle Obama on gender equality globally. From 2009 to 2013, Bigio was senior advisor to the U.S. ambassador-at-large for global women's issues at the Department of State and was detailed to the office of the undersecretary of defense for policy and the U.S. Mission to the African Union. Bigio led the interagency launch of the U.S. National Action Plan on Women, Peace, and Security, an effort for which she was recognized with the U.S. Department of State Superior Honor Award and the U.S. Department of Defense Secretary of Defense Honor Award. Prior to joining the U.S. government, Bigio worked for the United Nations in New York, Ethiopia, and Jordan, and for public health nongovernmental organizations in Ethiopia. Bigio graduated from the University of Maryland and received her master's degree from the Harvard Kennedy School.

Rachel B. Vogelstein is the Douglas Dillon senior fellow and director of the Women and Foreign Policy program at the Council on Foreign Relations. From 2009 to 2012, Vogelstein was director of policy and senior advisor within the office of U.S. Secretary of State Hillary Clinton and represented the U.S. Department of State as a member of the White House Council on Women and Girls. Previously, Vogelstein was the director of the women and girls' programs in the office of Hillary Clinton at the Clinton Foundation, where she oversaw the development of the No Ceilings initiative and provided guidance on domestic and global women's issues. Prior to joining the State Department, Vogelstein was senior counsel at the National Women's Law Center in Washington, DC, where she specialized in women's health and reproductive rights. Vogelstein is a recipient of the U.S. Department of State Superior Honor Award and a National Association of Women Lawyers award. She graduated from Barnard College and received a law degree from the Georgetown University Law Center.

STUDY GROUP
Ending Modern Slavery in the Twenty-First Century

Luis C. deBaca
*Former Ambassador-at-Large
to Monitor and Combat Human
Trafficking, 2009-2014*

Jean Baderschneider
*Global Fund to End Modern
Slavery*

Sharan Burrow
*International Trade Union
Confederation*

Kevin Cassidy
International Labor Organization

James Cockayne
*Liechtenstein Initiative for Finance
Against Slavery and Trafficking;
University of Nottingham
CFR Study Group Chair*

Susan Coppedge
*Former Ambassador-at-Large
to Monitor and Combat Human
Trafficking, 2015–2017*

Minh Dang
Survivor Alliance

Karrie Denniston
Walmart.org

Cindy Dyer
Vital Voices Global Partnership

Nancy H. Ely-Raphel
*Former Ambassador-at-Large
to Monitor and Combat Human
Trafficking, 2001-2002*

Susan G. Esserman
*University of Maryland SAFE
Center*

Marcy Forman
Citi

Maria Grazia Giammarinaro
*Former Special Rapporteur on
Trafficking in Persons, Especially
Women and Children*

Nick Grono
Freedom Fund

Siddharth Kara
*Carr Center for Human Rights
Policy, Harvard Kennedy School*

Mark P. Lagon
*Former Ambassador-at-Large
to Monitor and Combat Human
Trafficking, 2007–2009*

Philip Langford
International Justice Mission

Earl Lewis
University of Michigan

Shawn MacDonald
Verité

Cindy Hensley McCain
The McCain Institute

Sarah E. Mendelson
Carnegie Mellon University

Nadia Murad
Nadia's Initiative

Randy Newcomb
The Omidyar Group

Sophie Otiende
*Awareness Against Human
Trafficking*

Anesa Parker
Deloitte Consulting LLP

Stewart M. Patrick
Council on Foreign Relations

Anita Ramasastry
*University of Washington School
of Law*

Fiona Reynolds
*Principles for Responsible
Investment*

Laura C. Rubbo
The Walt Disney Company

Martina E. Vandenberg
*The Human Trafficking Pro Bono
Legal Center*

Jay Vann
U.S. Coast Guard

Rob Wainwright
Deloitte Risk Advisory B.V.

Bukeni Waruzi
Free the Slaves
